Niq Mhlongo

Affluenza

Kwela Books

KWELA Books,
an imprint of NB Publishers,
a division of Media24 Boeke (Pty) Ltd,
40 Heerengracht, Cape Town, South Africa
www.kwela.com

Copyright © 2016 Niq Mhlongo

All rights reserved
No part of this book may be reproduced or transmitted in any form
or by any electronic or mechanical means, including photocopying and
recording, or by any other information storage retrieval system,
without written permission from the publisher

Cover design by Russell Starcke
Typography by Nazli Jacobs
Set in 9.5 on 15.5pt Utopia
Printed and bound by Capitil Press,
Paarden Eiland, South Africa

First edition, first impression 2016
Second impression 2016

ISBN: 978-0-7957-0696-7
ISBN: 978-0-7957-0697-4 (epub)
ISBN: 978-0-7957-0698-1 (mobi)

CONTENTS

The Warning Sign	7
Goliwood Drama	16
The Dark End of Our Street	27
Four Blocks Away	32
Betrayal in the Wilderness	48
Catching the Sun	56
My Name is Peaches	79
The Gumboot Dancer	94
The Baby Shower	113
Affluenza	126
Passport and Dreadlocks	143
Acknowledgements	192

THE WARNING SIGN

When a stone hit the roof of his house with a thunderous clatter, Mr Adams knew they had come for him. It was around four in the morning and still dark outside. Panicking, he retrieved the rifle that he always kept under his bed and tiptoed towards the window barefoot.

"Kaffirs! What do these monkeys think they would be without us white people?"

Pressing his forehead against the cold glass, he looked outside, the rifle ready in his hands.

"Lazy bastards! If it wasn't for us you would still be living in mud huts."

Outside, his dogs began to bark.

"Come on, you cowards! I'll slit your throats! You devils! You scoundrels!" he said with his face still pressed against the windowpane.

Mr Adams was a well-built man in his mid-sixties. He was still strong, married with four children – three sons and a daughter. His eldest son, Ben, was in his early forties. His daughter Joan, the youngest of his children, was in her mid-twenties. Joan and her mother, his wife Ann, were on vacation indefinitely in Cape Town, at their holiday home. Mr Adams had insisted that they leave the farm after the family had received a visit from a group calling themselves the Land Redistribution Committee of Mzansi.

For the past five days Mr Adams and his sons had been patrolling the farm. They knew who the intruders were and they knew exactly what they wanted.

Mr Adams spoke fluent Shona and always employed Shona-speaking people as his workforce. His favourite were the Zezuru. According to him, they were hard workers. His family had had Zezuru workers on their farms around Gweru some years earlier. That was before they were forced to flee to South Africa, during the land grab in 2000. Mr Adams never paid well, but then there were always unemployed Zimbabweans out there who would jump at an opportunity to come and work for him. He made sure that every Monday he personally collected his Shona workforce from Beitbridge. He would then drive back to his farm between Bela-Bela and Thabazimbi with them in the back of his bakkie. Part of the deal was that they got a free place to stay for the week, in the workers' accommodation that was a couple of kilometres from the main house, but these days they never lasted long. Sometimes a day or two days, but by Wednesday or Thursday they would be gone. They would just disappear in the middle of the night. Mr Adams had no idea where they went, but he suspected that they went to look for better opportunities in Johannesburg.

Mr Adams's trusted farm manager, Knowledge, was the latest to disappear. Of his Shona workforce, he was now left with only three ladies: Patience, Memory and Grace. They stayed closer to the house, in the servants' quarters just outside the perimeter fence.

The dogs continued barking outside. Mr Adams peered out onto the driveway. All he could see was the big water tank and a host of shadowy figures created by his own imagination.

"You are trespassing," he heard one of his sons shout out into the darkness. "I will shoot you dead!"

Anger welled up in Mr Adams. His chest heaved like that of an asthmatic and he began to blink rapidly to clear his eyes of the water that kept forming from gazing so intently out through the glass.

Two hours later, the sun touched the tips of the trees on the eastern edge of the farm.

As soon as it was light, Mr Adams and his sons decided to inspect the farm. George, his second born, was left to guard the house while Mr Adams, James, his youngest son, and Ben ventured out beyond the perimeter fence. The three of them took different routes, each armed with a rifle. James took the sweet potato and tomato fields. Mr Adams went to the other side of the stream, where they had planted cabbages and potatoes. Ben covered the orange orchard and the land beneath the mountain where there was a small herd of cattle. They agreed to meet at twelve for lunch at the dam. The dam was near the stream and was fenced to prevent the crocodiles that they reared there from crawling out.

Mr Adams stopped and peered down at the footpath, examining a footprint. He was pale and there were dark signs of sleeplessness beneath his eyes. Suspiciously, he looked around him. All he could see was a ridge of ploughed land with an abandoned tractor upon it. It had been left there by Knowledge the day before he disappeared. He followed the footprints, his boots rustling through the dry leaves, until he came to a pole with a demarcation sign nailed to it. It read:

PROPERTY OF THE LAND REDISTRIBUTION
COMMITTEE OF MZANSI

The sight of the sign left an unpleasant taste in his mouth. He pressed his chin into the collar of his khaki shirt, an action that gave his face an expression of displeasure. "Kaffirs!" he said as he began removing the sign. "What the fuck do they know about farming? The only thing they know how to grow is babies!"

Frowning and clenching his jaw, Mr Adams carried on walking, the sign in his hand. He knew that it had been placed there by the group of men and women that had come to his farm uninvited a week earlier.

"If it were not for us white people these monkeys would still be praying to their clueless ancestors. They would have no idea of the vast mineral wealth below the soil."

Mr Adams sat down in the dappled shade provided by an acacia tree, his rifle across his knees. Bees hovered over the brightly coloured flowers that protruded from the tree and the sound of them going about their business began to lull him to sleep. As he dozed under the tree his mind began replaying the events of the previous week.

"I'm in charge of the land which Mr Rens, your neighbour, used to own," one of the men, the one with a limp, had said. "I'm the commander of the land committee."

"What does that have to do with me?" Mr Adams had asked.

"Your farm is next. My men will come and survey your land next week. Then you will be required to take your things and go."

"That is not the way things are done here. This is not Zimbabwe. There is a rule of law," Mr Adams had protested slowly and scornfully. "You can't simply take people's land without paying for it."

"The soil is ours. We have no obligation to pay you compensation. You stole the land from us just like the Americans stole the land from the Native Americans, the Australians from the aborigines."

"What you are trying to do is illegal and unconstitutional. You can't just pick and choose which laws to obey. People like Mandela fought so that we could all live peacefully."

"Mandela was a traitor. You settlers took the land from us without paying for it centuries ago. Why should we entertain any ideas of legality?"

"I paid for this land. Nothing is free in this world."

"Mandela's weakness was that he wanted to act morally and legally when your ancestors acted immorally and illegally."

"But he created a spirit of reconciliation and forgiveness, he created the rainbow nation."

"Fuck that! There is no black in the rainbow."

"But I bought this land. I have a title deed. Where do you think I must go?"

"We don't care!" the commander had said, his gaze unflinching. "This is our land. You white settlers took the land from us without paying for it. We can, in a similar way, take it back from you without paying for it."

"Can't there be peace in this country?" Mr Adams had exclaimed.

"You can't separate peace from land. No white person will be at peace until the land is returned to the people."

By that time Mr Adams's sons had arrived.

"What's going on, Pops?" George had asked.

"We all have the right to live here," Mr Adams had said, ignoring his son. "Historically, there were no black people here when white people arrived in the early sixteen hundreds. The Ngunis were all in northern KwaZulu, Mpumalanga, Swaziland and Mozambique. The Xhosas were in the Eastern Cape, across the Fish River. And the Pedis were all living in caves around Sekhukhuneland. You have no right to claim this land. Just because you are black doesn't mean that you have a blank cheque for this entire region."

"This is the land of our ancestors and we farmed here before you whites came."

"You can't blame us for what our ancestors did to your ancestors," James had said. "We . . ."

The sound of a car passing on the main road to Bela-Bela interrupted Mr Adams's daydream. Birds had settled in the tree above him and his two ridgebacks had curled up at his feet. As a breeze began to blow the birds took off, filling the air with their carolling, and the two ridgebacks burst out barking. Filled with fear, Mr Adams stood and brought his rifle to his shoulder.

"Come get me, you cowards! This is my farm!" His voice was loud and the words tumbled out. "You're not getting shit out of it!"

The sun was at its height when Mr Adams reached the dam. His breathing sounded forced and the combination of anger and heat had made his face as red as an overripe tomato.

"The bastards were here last night," Mr Adams said, throwing the sign he had taken down at his sons' feet, his skin glistening with sweat.

"Are you okay, Pops?" asked Ben with concern on his face.

"I will be fine." His lips quivered a little. "I told you: they're all cowards, these bastards! They must come during the day and fight like men."

Mr Adams joined his sons where they were standing at the fence by the dam, watching the crocodiles. The water was muddy and brown.

"Bloody kaffirs!" Mr Adams swore as he looked down on the crocodiles, writhing and tumbling in the dam.

That afternoon George called the police. They promised to come and investigate, but by eight in the evening they still hadn't arrived at the house. After trying to get through to the station several times, Mr Adams was told that the police were understaffed and had twenty or more similar cases around the Bela-Bela area. Fifteen farms had already been occupied.

That night, around eleven, Grace was woken by muffled screams. Opening her curtain, she saw three figures dragging Knowledge's wife, Memory, from her quarters.

At about five the following morning Mr Adams was woken by the bark of a jackal. Sitting up, he looked quickly around him, then reached for his rifle that was standing next to his bed.

Outside, the trees were swaying menacingly in the wind and the moon was covered by low-hanging clouds. The black wall of the forest seemed closer than Mr Adams remembered, as he peered from his window, but otherwise everything was quiet.

Mr Adams whistled to his sons.

"What is it, Pops?" George asked.

"Something is going on," Mr Adams replied. "Take your positions, boys."

As if on cue, the dogs began to bark. Men and women were surrounding the farmhouse, chanting slogans.

All the veins on Mr Adams's neck stood out as soon as he heard the noise, fear beginning to brew in the pit of his stomach. As the crowd continued to approach the perimeter fence he opened the window and fired off a warning shot.

"Over my dead body! You people cannot take my farm!" His voice was full of forced bravery. "We have title deeds."

Meanwhile George was busy trying to call the police – his cell phone in one hand and his gun in the other – and James was loading his rifle.

As Ben took his position at the back of the house two shots rang out, one of them smashing the kitchen window. He bravely kicked open the back door and started randomly shooting into the crowd. A woman went down, shot in the shoulder. She screamed, rolling her eyes and tearing at the earth in pain.

In response several shots cracked out, one after the other. One of the bullets pierced George's chest and Mr Adams looked on in horror as his second born fell to the floor bleeding. Clutching his wound, George tried to reach his cell phone, which he had dropped when the bullet had hit him, but he slipped into unconsciousness before he could wrap his hand around it.

The sky was already bright when the police finally arrived. Mr Adams's face was as white as chalk and his hair was caked with blood, which had also stained his khaki shirt. All his sons were lying face down, dead. A trail of blood led from the kitchen, down the passageway and into the lounge, showing the path Ben had taken before he finally collapsed next to his dying father. Meanwhile, outside, the comrades were tending to their wounded and dead, of which there were many. None of the comrades had tried to call the police as they were aware of how the latter operated. They knew that the police deliberately took their time whenever guns were involved.

Yellow police tape fluttered in the hot breeze, the colour lurid against the house's ivy-clad walls. The police had found Mr Adams's arsenal – explosives and automatic weapons – after questioning Patience and Grace. They had also found the human bones at the dam – Mr Adams had never been able to work out why the crocodiles grew so big so fast.

GOLIWOOD DRAMA

Soweto

The time was 16:00, according to the big clock at the Mangalani BP garage. If you were not from around Chiawelo you would think the time shown was correct, but the locals were aware that the "BP watch" was ahead of time by almost thirty minutes. That Saturday, 15 March, 16:30, the sky above Soweto was about to be ripped apart by fireworks. It was a day that would remind many Sowetans of the day Mandela was released from jail after spending twenty-seven years behind bars.

Thirty-nine-year-old Thami ducked involuntarily as the first set of explosions went off. His friend Vusi also flinched. They had been sitting on the balcony of their favourite Chiawelo shebeen – 24HOURS – since two o'clock that afternoon. They were not drunk yet, just tipsy, although Vusi had bulging, bloodshot eyes that could easily be mistaken for those of a drunken man. He was a lawyer by profession and had offices in Joburg. Thami worked as one of the cabinet minister's bodyguards. Many people in the township called him "The Bull" because of his massive body.

24HOURS was filled with people and all eyes were glued to the TV that was mounted on the wall above the bar. There was no music playing. Everyone was waiting eagerly. Some people were biting their nails in anticipation. A very important announcement was about to be made by the FIFA President, Sepp Blatter. Everyone was hoping that South Africa would be selected ahead of Tunisia to host the World Cup in 2010.

Thami, meanwhile, felt alone, even amongst the throng of people in 24HOURS. He looked like he was enjoying his Castle Lager, the way he sipped it slowly and licked his thick lips. And, of course, he was in good company – his best friend Vusi was by his side. But Thami's heart was heavy. His mind was busy, racing like a moth looking for a flame. Less than two months earlier he had separated from Thuli, his common-law wife of eight years. He could not believe that he would be facing her at the Johannesburg Maintenance Court that coming Monday.

"Just look at me, man. Everyone can tell that I'm as black as Africa itself. I cannot be that boy's real father. There is no history of albinos in my family," said Thami. He paused and took a drag from his cigarette. "Thuli probably slept with an albino guy when I was away with The Chief."

"Stop it, man!" said Vusi, shaking his head. "These things happen. There is probably a biological reason."

"Balls!" said Thami. "Even my mother knows that kid is not mine. I'm going to tell the court on Monday that I can't pay maintenance for the kid when I know he's not mine."

"I've advised you to deny paternity in the court on Monday, so what are you still worried about?"

"I'm going to miss all the celebrations because of that stupid court case. Everybody from Parliament will be at the presidential residence if South Africa wins the bid, from the Governor of the Reserve Bank to the Minister of Sport."

At that very moment a joyful noise filled the tavern. South Africa had just been declared the host of the 2010 FIFA World Cup! People were hugging each other. From where they sat, Thami and Vusi could even see cars on the Old Potchefstroom Road flashing their headlights in celebration.

"You see, baba," said Vusi proudly, "if you want to watch a movie you don't have to travel to town. Our Soweto is like Hollywood and Bollywood combined. Viva 2010 World Cup, viva!" He burped loudly after sipping from his quart of Castle Lager.

"Oh, sure," Thami answered uninterestedly, flicking the ash of his cigarette onto the floor.

"Come on. Don't give me that look," said Vusi, a mixture of pity and disappointment on his face. "You can do better than that."

Thami did not say a word. Instead he stared at the empty bottle he was holding as if he were wishing it full again. From every direction came the deafening sound of vuvuzelas and the hooting of the cars. Nearby, some thugs started spinning their BMWs. A huge crowd of people, young and old, watched in amazement. It looked as if the whole of Soweto had come out onto the street to celebrate.

Monday morning

Thami was driving along the M1 North in his Honda Ballade, heading for the centre of Joburg. The traffic was moving very slowly, as usual. Thami looked at the clock on the dashboard. It was half past nine. He began to panic. His friend Vusi had warned him a number of times about the magistrate at the maintenance court. "She will not hesitate to hold you in contempt of court for not showing up on time," he had said.

To Thami's relief, the traffic started to ease near Gold Reef casino, cars began to move faster. The road was like that until he arrived at the court, four minutes before his case was due to start.

Inside, the benches were crowded. Most of the people there were women. As he entered, Thami spotted Thuli. Her face was almost beautiful, she had great bone structure, but her flat nose spoiled her looks. Her hair was well braided and her Police sunglasses were pushed back on her forehead. She wore a Gucci leather jacket and big silver earrings dangled from both her ears.

Thuli could not hide her anger as she saw Thami approach.

"And you call yourself a man? I don't think so!" said Thuli out loud as she got to her feet. She shook her head. "Do you want me to tell you what real men do, huh? Real men support their children. They put bread on the table every day for their children. Real men pay for their children's studies, and they make sure that their children have shelter. You are not a real man because you do not support your children."

"Yes. Tell the bastard how he is," said a lady who was breastfeeding a baby on the opposite bench.

Thami was tight-lipped. Everyone in the corridor was looking at him. He felt humiliated.

Thuli clicked her tongue twice and wrinkled her nose. There was an expression of bitterness on her face. "Just look at you!" she eyed him sharply. "You are not even ashamed of yourself! You are here wearing an expensive suit and nice shoes but your three children are naked and barefoot at home. I would be ashamed of myself if I were you."

"Divorce the bastard and get on with your life, girl. You are still young and there are lots of men out there that would kill to be with you," said another woman who was sitting at the far end of the bench. Leaning forward she snapped her fingers. "Just like that! Dump him like a hot potato, girl. But you must make sure the bastard pays heavily for wasting your precious time."

Thami pinched his nose. Many thoughts were going through his mind.

"Your friends think that you're a man because you are Deputy President Zuma's bodyguard." Thuli shook her head again. "I don't think so. They might mistake you for a man because of that useless stick between your legs, but you are not a man!"

There was laughter from the women sitting on the benches around him. Thami was tempted to retaliate, but he remembered Vusi's advice that he should be civil to everyone in the court at all times. At the same time, the door to one of the offices yawned open. A woman in black pants and a blue shirt appeared. On the door was written: *Ms Dube, Marriage Counsellor.*

"Mr and Mrs Maphela!" the woman in black pants called out as the noise in the corridor subsided. "Come to my office, please."

Thuli and Thami followed the woman inside. She pushed the door shut and gestured to them to sit in the two chairs provided as she took her place behind her desk. Above Ms Dube's head was a poster with the words *Stop the violence against women and children* splashed across it. Below it was a framed photograph of a woman shaking President Thabo Mbeki's hand. Thami realised that it was a picture of the woman who was sitting before them.

"Well, as you might already know, my name is Sylvia Dube," said the woman. There was an authoritative tone in her voice. "I am the marriage counsellor. I can tell that it's a difficult period for the two of you. I also know that, for the sake of the children, Mrs Maphela here has laid a complaint against you, Mr Maphela, for not providing financial support." Her eyes moved from Thuli to Thami. "I understand that you are earning the same amount as before you split from your wife, so why are you not paying maintenance, Mr Maphela? Why are you not supporting your children anymore?"

"You are right, counsellor. The problem is not money. I am denying paternity of the last born. I don't believe I fathered him," said Thami, forcing calmness into his voice. Despite the fact that his words were the truth, he regretted them the moment they were out of his mouth. He loved his two older children and was worried about how everything that had happened might have affected them. He had only stopped paying maintenance because of the last born.

"What?" Thuli demanded angrily. "You want to tell me that all the years we were together you didn't trust me? And, not only that, you didn't have the balls to face me? Is that right?"

Thami remained calm. He did not say a word.

"Hold on! Let me get this straight," said Counsellor Dube. "You are saying that you are here to contest the paternity of one of your children, is that right?"

"Right."

"Are you sure about this?"

"Yes, I am. My intuition tells me that the last born is not mine. I want to clear it up once and for all," said Thami.

"What about the other two? Why are you not supporting them?"

"I am sorry for my behaviour. This whole thing has affected me deeply and I am aware that I haven't been making good decisions."

"Did it affect you to the extent that you failed to support your own children?"

"Yes. I guess so."

"So you want a paternity test?" asked Counsellor Dube.

"Yes, that's what I want. I want to clear my doubts. And if in fact I am the father, I will happily support my child."

"You are a liar! You are not doing this for the sake of the children," interrupted Thuli angrily, looking at Thami like she could plunge her long nails into his face.

"Mrs Maphela, let's –"

"Please, call me Thuli. I no longer want to be associated with his surname."

"Okay, Thuli. We assure you that this court will do everything in its power to make sure that your children are well looked after," said Counsellor Dube, trying to calm her down.

"Why are you running away from your responsibilities?" shouted Thuli impatiently, turning on Thami, her eyes searching his face. "You might as well forget about it. I don't need your money. You can keep your dirt. The children and I can survive without your help. You must forget about us, we don't need you in our lives anymore."

Counsellor Dube looked at her watch. "I'm just going next door to consult the magistrate," she said, standing up with some papers in her hand. "I'll be back in a minute. I want you two to behave when I'm gone. Don't shout at each other inside my office."

Not a single word was spoken between Thuli and Thami while Counsellor Dube was out of the room. They even shied away from looking at each other. Thami's eyes remained downcast; Thuli tapped her fingers on the table rhythmically. They remained like that until Counsellor Dube returned ten minutes later.

"Both of you will be appearing before the magistrate in room four in about thirty minutes," said Counsellor Dube. "I had thought that this was only about maintenance, but it is obviously more complex than that. I don't have the authority to order a paternity test, but the magistrate has. Oh . . ." She paused as if trying to soften the blow that was to come. "The unfortunate part of it is that all five of you . . . I mean you and your three children, will all have to undergo the test. We want to compare all your DNA and make sure that the outcome of the test is a hundred per cent correct. Are there any questions that either of you would like to ask?"

Thuli shook her head. "No. I am sorry, but I can't subject my children to this torture because he has some crazy idea that our last born is not his."

"Unfortunately," said Counsellor Dube, "the matter is now in the hands of this court. And this court is required by law to resolve any matters brought before it."

Thirty minutes later Thami and Thuli appeared in front of the magistrate. The hearing lasted only ten minutes as Thami maintained his original position. A court order was issued by the magistrate requiring Thami and Thuli, as well as their three children, to go to the nearest laboratory and have their blood taken. The next court date was in two weeks' time.

24HOURS

Thami tried to catch the waitress's attention by waving his right hand. He was thirsty for another beer. As soon as the waitress came, he gave her a fifty-rand note and ordered two Castle Lager quarts. Most people were watching the derby between Kaizer Chiefs and Orlando Pirates.

"Pirates have to win this game if they are serious about winning the league this year," said Thami.

"I think today is Pirates' day, man. They are playing well."

The waitress came with two beers and put them on their table. Vusi opened one of the bottles with his teeth. "The next round will be on me," he said as he poured beer into his glass.

"Thanks, man," said Thami and laughed sadly. "Very soon I'll not be able to afford to buy you a beer, my friend. All my money will be going on maintenance."

"When are you going to know the outcome of all of this?" asked Vusi.

"The day after tomorrow."

"What are you going to do if it turns out that all the children are yours?"

"I'm ready for any result, man. Whatever comes, I'll have to act like a man."

Friday morning
Magistrate Zodwa Khumalo was to preside over the court proceedings. Their case was due to start at nine o'clock, but both Thami and Thuli arrived early. Thuli was accompanied by her mother and her best friend. Thami had come with Vusi. There

were already about twenty people seated on the benches inside the courtroom. Everybody remained quiet.

"This is the case of paternity between Thami and Thuli Maphela," said Magistrate Khumalo after clearing her throat. "May the two parties step forward, please."

Vusi gave his friend a big wink and raised his thumb.

"We will start with Leleti Maphela, a female, born on 17 July 1997. For the case of paternity you brought before this court, you are excused. You are not the father," said the magistrate, looking at her files.

Thami's palms began to sweat as he took in what the magistrate was saying.

"The second child, Zolani Maphela, a male, born on 10 October 2000. For the case of paternity, the court excuses you as the father."

Thami swallowed deeply.

"The third child is Zandi Maphela, a female, born on 2 January 2003. For the case of paternity, you are the father. You are therefore required by this court to maintain your child by paying the amount of seven hundred and fifty rand every month."

24HOURS

The shebeen was crowded. It was Friday evening. Thami and Vusi were seated in a corner, next to a large speaker that was blaring out Kamazu's classic "Korobela".

> *African woman, why give me korobela?*
> *Oh, korobela.*

Thami sang along to the song, his head moving rhythmically to the music.

"This song speaks to me, man. I think Thuli gave me a love potion to blind me. How else is it possible that I didn't see that she was cheating on me all along?" asked Thami as the song ended.

"Don't blame yourself, man," said Vusi. "I've heard that most women use it on their men. My father told me that they apply it to their arms, thighs and genitals before sex. When a man is busy dancing between his woman's legs and enjoying it, the potion is transferred."

"You see me married again, you cut my throat. I have had enough of women," said Thami drunkenly.

THE DARK END OF OUR STREET

"Do you recognise the handwriting?" Detective Nkosi asked Sipho.

Detective Nkosi was one of three police officers in what had until very recently been Sbu's Leo Marquard Residence room. The second police officer, Detective Nhlapo, and Uncle George (Sbu's uncle) were busy packing Sbu's belongings into two large cardboard boxes. The third officer, Detective Sithole, was standing on the balcony. He was busy making some measurements from where they thought Sbu had jumped to his death the previous night.

Sipho looked at the piece of paper that had been handed to him by Detective Nkosi. He was convinced that the writing belonged to his friend. They had almost everything in common: they had started at the University of Cape Town in the same year, attended the same courses and stayed at the same residence. They had often compared lecture notes, but when Sipho looked at the words in front of him, it was as if the person who had written them was drunk or under the influence of some drug.

"Well . . ." Sipho started in a stammering voice. "I think it is Sbu's writing."

"Are you sure?"

He looked at the paper again.

"Yes . . ."

"What makes you so sure?"

"Because we used to lend each other our lecture notes every Friday, and I'm quite used to the way he writes."

At that moment Sipho was struck by the fact that 13 November, that very day, was supposed to have been the day they celebrated Sbu's twenty-third birthday. He was convinced that his friend hadn't expected to die. It had to be a mistake. The previous afternoon, Sbu had even proposed a party to celebrate his birthday and the end of exams. If he knew that he was going to commit suicide, why then would he invite all of his friends to come to his birthday party the following day?

"Did your friend have any enemies?" asked Detective Nkosi.

"I don't think so. Why?"

"Was your friend suffering from depression?"

"I don't think so."

"Was he expecting any visitors after you?"

"I don't know."

"What about his girlfriend? Do you know her, by any chance?"

"Yes," Sipho said doubtfully, "but as far as I know they were no longer going out. They broke up last month."

"Aha, is that so?"

"Yes, as far as I know."

"Did you know that she was here yesterday?"

"Who, Zanele? Was she?"

"By looking at his suicide note, do you suspect that Sbu was under some form of pressure when he wrote it?"

"Well, I can't tell that. But I can't rule out the possibility either."

"Look carefully. The words are not exactly between the lines. Can you see? Did he sometimes used to write like this?"

"Only when he was in a hurry, during note-taking in class."

"Thanks a lot for your time," said Detective Nkosi, handing his card to Sipho. "Please let us know if you think of anything that might help our investigation into this matter."

The following morning, Sipho didn't get up. He had no idea how he had managed to walk to his room the previous afternoon, but his body felt heavy, as if he had been carrying bags of cement the whole night. It was even difficult to open his eyes. He turned over; his stomach felt empty, but he had lost his appetite the moment he had received the news of his friend's death.

As Sipho slept a shaft of midday sunlight penetrated his room, roasting him. He had forgotten to close the curtains when he had come back from talking to the police.

Suddenly, he heard a knock on the door, followed by someone calling his name.

"I know you are there, Sipho. It's me, Zanele. Please open the door."

Sipho shifted the sheets and rolled to the other side of the bed. Some tobacco fell out of the pocket of the old brown leather jacket that he was still wearing as he stood and realised for the first time that he had slept with his shoes on. As he walked to the door he noticed a can of Black Label lying on its side on the floor. The whole room smelt of stale beer.

Zanele was carrying a blue sports bag with the varsity logo on it. She was studying at the drama school and was in her second year, but she had deferred all her remaining exams the previous day after hearing of the death of her ex-boyfriend.

"Hi," she said. "What smells so awful?"

"Eish. Maybe it's the beer..."

Sipho walked to the window and opened it.

"You know, I've been here since eleven this morning, and I've knocked on your door several times."

"I'm sorry. I didn't hear you," Sipho said, yawning.

"If it wasn't for the security guy downstairs who insisted that you were in, I would have left without seeing you."

Sipho went to the kitchen and plugged in the kettle to make coffee. The sink was full of dirty dishes and pots that had remained unwashed for about a week, and as he opened the fridge for some fresh milk Sipho could smell that the eggs had spoiled. He ignored the smell and took out the milk.

With a mug of coffee in each hand, he went back to his room. Zanele was sitting on his bed.

"When I saw that bag I thought that you were coming to give me a beer to kill this babalas," Sipho said, trying to make a joke.

There was silence for a while inside the room. A rill of slow-moving tears rolled down Zanele's brown cheek. She slowly wiped it away with the back of her hand.

"Sipho, can you do me a favour, please?"

"You know that you can always count on me."

"This bag belonged to Sbu. He gave it to me last night. I still had some of his things from when we were together, and he wanted me to drop them with him this morning. I'm asking you to give it to his family."

"So, you were with him before he died?"

"Yes." Zanele paused, the look on her face unreadable. "Why? What are people saying?"

"Nothing. I just hear rumours that you were in Sbu's room yesterday, before he died."

"Well, they aren't rumours. It's the truth."

Zanele finished her coffee and prepared to leave.

"Please, Sipho," she said as she stood up. "Just do this one thing for me. Make sure this bag gets back to Sbu's family."

"I'll see what I can do."

Sipho started to search the bag as soon as Zanele had left. Inside he found a washing rag, a pair of underpants, some books, a toothbrush and an envelope with a letter inside. The envelope was postmarked 11 November and was from Johannesburg Hospital. Opening it, Sipho could not believe his eyes when he read the word *Positive* in the *Status* section.

FOUR BLOCKS AWAY

My left eye was twitching nonstop. I'd been taught that this was a good sign. It meant that I was going to see something big. That is what my mother always used to say to me whenever my left eye went into spasm. Just like when the palm of my left hand was itchy. That was supposed to mean that I was going to come into a huge sum of money. Unless I scratched it – in which case my fortune would disappear.

Looking back, I have to say that my itchy palm never led to me receiving any money, but my twitchy eye often preceded pornographic horrors. I used to share a bedroom with my cousin Spice in Chi, Soweto, and on several occasions after my eye had been giving me trouble I woke up in the middle of the night to witness him naked on top of a woman he had snuck into our shared bedroom from the nearest shebeen.

So this is why, at the mature age of thirty-three, I still believed that my twitchy eye meant that I was going to see something big. However, I never figured on it happening while I was so far away from home. In the Hilton Hotel in Washington D.C., to be exact.

That Saturday the twitch was almost unbearable and my mind was filled with the things I might see. Part of me was hoping to bump into the various big shot South Africans who I'd heard had flown in to congratulate the newly elected president, Barack Obama.

I'd been in the US for about six months on a cultural exchange programme, teaching gumboot dancing to kids at the various schools around Iowa City. So, the fact that our visit to D.C., which was only for three days, had coincided with the inauguration of the first African-American president was extraordinary and wonderful.

Everyone from the programme was in D.C., including my two friends: Kuri, from Mutare in Zimbabwe, who taught mbira, and Bakala, from Bamako in Mali, who taught tabale. Kuri was in his mid-twenties, very thin and very tall. He looked like he didn't eat enough, which confirmed the idea that most people had about Zimbos around that time: that Mugabe was starving them to death. Bakala was older, in his early fifties, and almost always wore traditional dress. The three of us had stayed in the same house in Lynn Street back in Iowa City. Despite our different ages and backgrounds we had developed a close friendship and used to go shopping together at Coralville Mall.

We were all in D.C. to thank our generous sponsor, the Bureau of Educational and Cultural Affairs, for the unique opportunity they had provided us with, but that Saturday morning was our own time and we had decided to use it to explore D.C. At about nine we met in the lobby of the Hilton. Outside, the grey sky hung so low I felt I could reach out and touch it. It looked like it was going to rain.

My eye was still giving me trouble, so I decided to tell Kuri what my mother had always said when it started to twitch. Immediately, he suggested that we should give the White House a miss. "That twitching of yours means trouble, man," he teased. "The Ku Klux Klan is probably planning to bomb the new president!"

Just after three o'clock that afternoon Kuri, Bakala and I arrived back at the hotel. We were tired of walking around and had given up before seeing the Korean and Vietnam War memorials. We had, however, managed to see the White House, or as my high school history teacher used to call it: "The house where God resides."

The three of us were scheduled to give a talk and a performance at Howard University at five o'clock. My topic was The gumboot dance and the South African migrant labour system.

My eye was still twitching and I could not properly set my mind to the talk at the university. After scanning *USA Today* and the *Washington Post* in the lobby, I decided to go to my room, which I shared with Bakala, and lie down and close my eyes, in the hope that this would help.

At five o'clock we found ourselves in one of Howard University's lecture theatres. It was there that my mother's wisdom was confirmed. Beautiful, large eyes. Auburn hair, shading to brown in colour, that hung down to her shoulders like mielie tassels. She had spotted me from the crowd and was waving wildly. Her name was Siri.

I had met Siri in George's Bar in Iowa City on the night the election results had been announced. She had just broken up with her boyfriend and was drowning her sorrows. The following day she invited me to the cottage she was renting on the banks of the Iowa River. She cooked us pasta while telling me how the river had burst its banks back in June – her cottage had been flooded and it still smelt of damp.

Siri was from Philadelphia, studying towards a degree in literature at the University of Iowa. From the day of the dinner up until I left for D.C. we spent a great deal of time together. We were overtly physically affectionate towards one another – I would take her forearm and kiss it and in return she would hold my hand when we were sitting together – but each time I wanted to be more romantic her answer was always the same: "I have had enough of men. Please, give me some time." Those were her exact words.

Every few days after that night in George's Bar, I would find myself at Siri's place. We would sit by the Iowa River as the sun went down, smoke Egyptian tobacco mixed with weed from her hubbly bubbly and talk about the euphoria around Obama. We code-named smoking weed "reading poetry", and after each "poetry session" I would piggyback Siri for a short distance. We both loved it and would laugh all the way to her cottage, where I would leave her by the door.

Now Siri was standing in front of me in a lecture theatre in D.C. What did she want? I asked myself as I felt the palms of both my hands growing moist.

"Hey, beautiful," I said as I hugged her and planted a kiss on her forehead. "You look absolutely gorgeous. Beyond words."

"Hi, handsome," she replied.

"What a pleasant surprise. How are you here? Are you stalking me?"

"Yes, I am. I called one of the girls who is responsible for your itinerary and asked her where you were. She told me that you had a talk here." She paused. "So here I am."

"That is so lovely." I struggled to keep my gaze steady. "Thanks for coming."

"I drove all the way from Philly to see you."

"How far is that?"

"About four hours."

"Wow! You drove that far to see me? To what do I owe this honour?"

She didn't answer. Instead, she slapped me lightly on the shoulder and went to sit down in the front row of the lecture theatre.

Time and again, throughout the talk, my eyes drifted towards her.

After the talk, Siri clapped loudly, as if I had uttered the most profound words that she had ever heard.

When we were all done, Siri suggested that we go to ChurchKey in McPherson Square. "They normally have a happy hour at seven," she said.

"Sure thing."

Kuri and Bakala joined us and we all climbed into Siri's brown Ford sedan and headed off to 14th NW and Rhode Island.

ChurchKey was across the street from the Ghana Café. Siri parked along 14th NW and led us into the joint and to a booth with long yellow vintage couches. Three black ladies and two guys were in the booth opposite us, chatting and laughing. Siri ordered a prosciutto and fig flatbread, something I had never heard of before. The rest of us settled on chicken wings. A few minutes later, the waiter came with the *Beer Bible*. It had over five hundred international beers listed in it.

I don't recall how many different beers I drank that evening, but

I still remember some of the names: Sierra Nevada, Schneider Weisse, Kipling Pale, Prima Pils, Christmas Ale, Hefeweizen and Mad Elf. I enjoyed them all and, after knocking back a few bottles, my heart was aflame when I looked at Siri. The blue of her eyes reminded me of the colour of the ocean at Zanzibar's Mercury Beach where I had once performed.

"So, I think I must come with you to the motherland," Siri said to me. "You made it sound amazing."

The sound of those words coming from her lips was so sweet that I had difficulty controlling my emotions.

"I know why you don't want to come with me to Mali," said Bakala, acting as if he was jealous. "It's because of that girl who asked all those stupid questions during my talk about tabale."

"You mean the one who asked you whether you have roads in Mali?"

"Exactly that one," he said, taking a swig of beer. "I think she discouraged you."

There was laughter. At the same time, a crowd of young people swarmed in and sat in one of the empty booths not far from us. When I looked at the time, I realised it was already half past seven. Thirty minutes into Happy Hour.

"But I liked your answer," Siri said. "And people believed you when you said that there aren't any roads and that the US ambassador to Mali travels around the country by swinging from tree to tree. They were not at all surprised."

A rupture of laughter followed. It was the loud laughter of the drunks. Siri drained her glass and the waiter came with another, different beer and a new glass that matched the beer.

"Man, I get these stereotypes about Africa a lot. Remember the guy I was sitting next to at the back of the bus on our way to Coralville Mall the other day?" Bakala paused and looked around the table. "The whole trip he was telling me about his friend from Gabon, called Pete. Even after I had told him several times that I was from Mali, and it was a different country, he still asked if I knew his friend." He took a swig from his glass before putting it down. "So, in the end, to shut him up, I told him that I did know Pete. And you know what he did? He gave me his number to give to Pete, so that Pete could call him."

"The other day, as I came out of Penn Station in New York, I tossed a dollar into one of the homeless people's hats," Kuri said. "I think he heard me speaking with my brother in Shona. He asked me where I was from, and when I told him I was from Zim, he returned my dollar, saying that Africa probably needed the money more than he did. I was shocked."

There was laughter. I knew everyone was now exaggerating their experiences, but we were having a great time. Siri was giggling as if she had inhaled laughing gas. I still didn't know what her plans were for that night. I thought that she would probably drive back to Philadelphia. In any case, I was sharing my hotel room with Bakala. He was way older than me and in my culture it is unthinkable to ask an older guy to give up his room so that a younger person can have some privacy with a girl. Kuri was also sharing – with Dede from Brazzaville – which meant that my only option was to pay for another room in the Hilton Hotel. Unfortunately, I had exhausted most of my stipend on beer and the money I was left with wasn't going to be enough.

An opportunity to discuss all of this came when Siri went to the bathroom. In conspiratorial tones, Kuri and Bakala asked me what I wanted to do about sleeping arrangements. With the help of the alcohol in my brain, I explained to them that I couldn't ask Bakala to vacate our room.

Bakala laughed. "Well, it is unthinkable in my culture that a man would not give up his bed if his brother had something like that to chew on."

Bakala then told Kuri that he was coming to sleep in his room if Siri decided to come back to the hotel with me. He also told me not to worry about Dede – he would explain everything.

A few minutes later Siri came out of the bathroom and the four of us wobbled drunkenly out of the ChurchKey. A light rain had started.

Driving back, we passed Thomas Circle Park. Our hotel was just a few metres away and, after paying for the underground parking, Kuri and Bakala left Siri and me in the parking lot. We smoked a joint and, feeling a bit high, went straight to my room on the eleventh floor.

Inside the room Siri ignored the two chairs and sat on the floor at the foot of my bed. I grabbed a couple of beers from the mini-bar and sat down next to her. It was just like our Iowa days. The only difference was that she didn't resist when I kissed her.

I don't know whether it was because of the dope and the alcohol, but when Siri decided to take a shower, she stood up and took her clothes off right there, in front of me. Walking lazily to the bathroom, she invited me to follow with a wave of her hand. I obliged, taking off my clothes as my hunger for her lithe body began to overwhelm me.

"Do you have a condom?" she asked, dishing me a smile from inside the shower.

For a moment, as I watched her under the water, I was speechless. "No, I don't," I finally whispered.

"No glove, no love," she said, pointing her finger at me and smiling. "I suggest you go down to the lobby and ask them."

"I'll do that."

"Most hotels sell them," she said, her eyes large and coquettish. "And don't be late."

"I'll never be late for your love, baby."

I hurriedly put on my boxers and hotel gown. No shoes – I was just going to the lobby and back. No big deal.

In the lobby, the doorman smiled at me and then told me that they had run out of condoms.

Fuck!

"Where is the nearest place I can get them?" I asked, obviously disappointed. "Do you have a garage nearby that is still open?"

"What's a garage?"

"Just tell me where I can buy condoms," I said.

"Okay, try the CVS," he replied, a wobbly smile on his face.

"Where is it?" I asked.

"It's four blocks from here. As you walk out of the door, turn right. You'll see a shop across the street with *CVS Pharmacy* written on the windows."

"Do you think they're still open?"

"It's twenty-four hours."

Luckily the rain had slowed to a drizzle, but the pavement was still wet and the wind was icy on my back. I was not deterred, however. I was still buzzing with the warmth of the dozen beers I had drunk and the joint I had smoked in the parking lot with Siri. As I walked along the road, the image of Siri naked in the shower kept flashing into my brain and very soon my boxer shorts became far too small for my erection that projected ahead of me like a stolen rhino horn.

I crossed the street and passed Thomas Circle Park. There was a huge statue of a man sitting with a rifle in his hands in the park. Next to the rifle man's statue was another of a standing woman. I had passed through the park during the day and had read the name on the statue: John Barry. There had been a few homeless people in the park and I had been surprised by this – I had always thought that there were no homeless people in America – but now the rain seemed to have chased them away.

I stopped at a street and waited for the robot to turn green for me. The sign on the other side of the street had K STR NW 1300 stamped on it. Looking around, I could see a post office but no pharmacy. This didn't worry me. In my head four blocks sounded like just around the corner.

Back home in Soweto, four blocks would mean that I started counting from my neighbour's house, and the fourth house would be my destination. Anyway, the doorman had said that I could walk. And I didn't want to go back to the room without condoms, lest Siri change her mind about entertaining my excited rhino horn. That's what I thought as the robot turned green for me and I stepped out onto the rough tar. "Four blocks! No glove, no love!

Four blocks! No glove, no love!" my addled brain was singing over and over again.

Passing the Hamilton Hotel, I saw some homeless people sheltering under a building ahead. Some were smoking and others drinking something. A taxi stopped in front of me, but I kept walking. "I am just going four blocks," I told the driver, who looked Ethiopian. Ahead of me, I could see the name of the next street: L STR NW.

To my relief, just after crossing the street I saw the CVS Pharmacy on my right. I walked until I got to the Balance Gym, where I waited for a break in the traffic so that I could cross the street.

Before I could cross the road, I heard a loud police siren. It was followed by the flashing of a blue light beside me. When I looked, I saw a white sedan with the word *POLICE* emblazoned across it in huge letters. It had stopped just a few metres in front of me.

As I crossed the road, I noticed what looked like a homeless man playing a mouth organ outside the pharmacy. He had his hat on the ground in front of him with a few coins in it.

Entering the shop, I walked towards the till. While I was asking one of the women there where I could find the condoms, two policemen entered the shop. Maybe they are coming to buy doughnuts, I thought to myself. I knew from the movies that American policemen loved doughnuts. But, instead, the police interrupted my conversation with the lady behind the till.

"You're not allowed to walk around dressed like that, sir," said one of them in a bellicose voice. He had huge shoulders and a small head.

"Why not, officer?" I asked.

"It's the law here in America, sir," he said, looking at me like a god admonishing a sinner. "It's the moral code. You need to dress properly, with shoes on. Plain and simple."

His enunciation of the word *sir* was loaded with sarcasm. It was as if he wanted to indicate exactly how unwelcome I was in Washington D.C.

"I'm sorry, I didn't know, officer," I said, looking at my gown and my bare feet. "All I want are condoms."

"You are not allowed to buy anything dressed like that, sir," the second policeman said, taking hold of the collar of my gown.

"But I just came to buy condoms, officer," I said, trying to suppress the feeling of irritation that rose up inside me as the policemen escorted me firmly out of the pharmacy. "I didn't know it's not allowed."

Outside the pharmacy the homeless man stopped playing his mouth organ as the policemen walked me a few paces from the door.

"Okay, I understand, officers," I said as soon as they let me go. "Let's make a deal. How about I give one of you guys ten dollars to buy me condoms? The lady said they are in aisle eleven. You can buy me the brand of your choice and keep the change. And then everyone will be happy. What do you say, officers?"

The second policeman's eyes flashed fire and brimstone, his nostrils flared. Oh no, here comes trouble! I thought to myself when I saw him balling his hands into fists. This is America. Black people are sent to jail over nothing.

"Where are you from?" the policeman asked angrily.

"Mzansi."

"Where the hell is that?"

"Africa. South Africa," I said.

He threw me a cold look as if it was an unpardonable sin for a South African to be in the United States.

"Are you here on holiday or business?"

"Arts."

"Who are you visiting, and how long have you known the person you are visiting?"

"Well, I don't know the person because she is in the American government."

"Does your government friend have a job title and an address?"

"Well, she is here somewhere, at the state department."

"Do you have family here in D.C.?"

"No. I'm Sowetan."

By this time a few passers-by had stopped to enjoy the drama. One large black lady had taken a front-line position as if she wanted to hear every word that was being exchanged between us. She gave me a broad smile that I could only translate to mean that she was on my side.

"Are you here for a green card?" asked the policeman with the small head through clenched teeth.

"What's a green card?" I asked, deliberately sounding as if I didn't know what he was talking about.

"Are you interested in staying here permanently or what?" he asked, his voice low with rage.

"Hell no! I just want to buy some condoms."

There was laughter.

"I'm sorry, but, as I already said, we can't allow you to buy anything dressed like that."

"Okay, I do understand, officers, but can't one of you help me out? I'm begging you! This American lady is waiting eagerly for me back at the hotel."

"What's wrong with these people?" I heard a big sister say to the small crowd that had now gathered. "Just give brother Kunta the fucking condoms. He just wanna taste some American nookie."

There was laughter again.

"May I see your papers, please?" said the second policeman, looking at me seriously. "How did you come to this country?"

"What?"

"May I see your papers." He spoke very slowly as if every word he said was costing him in American dollars.

"Well, I obviously don't have my papers with me. They are at the hotel."

"Where is your hotel?"

"Four blocks away, the Hilton."

"What's your name?"

"Qhawe Mcwabe."

The policemen looked amused at how my tongue clicked when I said my name and there and then a thought struck me.

"I am Qhawe Mcwabe," I repeated. "I'm Khambule, Mzilankatha, inkatha kayingen'endlini, yangena kubola izinkaba zabantwana."

The spectators started clapping. The policeman with the small head eyed me with a mixture of distrust and scepticism before shaking his head.

"What did you come here to do?"

"Well, I'm a mbongi and gumboot dancer. I have been sent by his majesty, our King back home, to come and congratulate President Obama on his election with some isiZulu praise poetry."

"You have to go back to your hotel and dress properly, sir."

"You are giving me no choice, officer. I will have to tell the audience during my praise poetry for President Obama that I was denied access to condoms. What is your name again, officer?"

There was laughter again. The policeman looked at me and I stared back at him.

"That's nonsense," the policeman finally said after a moment of uncertain silence.

"Do you mean my culture, or the condoms?"

"Okay, we'll let you in. But on condition that you go straight to aisle eleven and buy only the condoms."

"Thank you, officer," I said, bowing my head with the palms of my hands together. "I will remember your kindness back at the hotel."

"Just go before we change our minds."

The policemen's eyes never left me as I went to aisle eleven. The sign above it said *FAMILY PLANNING, INCONTINENCE, FEMININE HYGIENE*. Having made my choice, I went up to the till with the condoms and paid. As I turned back towards the door I saw that they were still standing and watching me.

"Enjoy, brother," said the big sister at the door as I made my way outside.

I smiled at her, savouring the thought of Siri naked back at the hotel. My senses were surging sweetly as I imagined her twenty-three-year-old body waiting to be devoured by my rhino horn.

By the time I got back to the hotel, Siri was sleeping. She was lying across the bed, snoring, her golden pubic hair glistening in the moonlight. I stared at her firm round breasts and the small butterfly tattoo on her hip while I tried to decide on the best way to wake her. Eventually, I opened the window and lit a joint. I thought that the smell might wake her. When it didn't, I shook her gently several times. She did not respond.

BETRAYAL IN THE WILDERNESS

We had spent the last three and a half hours tracking the Big Five in a reserve near the Kruger National Park. This was my Valentine's Day gift to my wife Mmabatho, mother of my three kids. We had been married for the past eight years and every year I had taken her away somewhere special on 14 February. She had hinted at a trip to Cape Town as the big day approached, talking of how much she wanted to visit Robben Island, but I had convinced her that she would enjoy the Kruger National Park after reading about it on the internet.

By five-thirty that afternoon we had seen elephant, lion, rhino and buffalo. The leopard, however, had successfully evaded us. As I watched, Xoli, our ranger and driver, and Nathi, his assistant and animal tracker, climbed out of the Land Rover to look for fresh prints in the dusty track.

"Is that you, Mr Leopard? Please, come out!" Mmabatho sang as something made a sound in the nearby bush. She waved her Sony camera above her head as if this would draw the creature out of hiding.

"Yes! Come out, Mr Leopard!" chorused the white woman sitting next to my wife as a startled warthog appeared and ran away down the track.

My wife has always had a habit of being a little too open with strangers. We had met the couple that were with us in the Land Rover, Andrea and Jean, the previous night during dinner, but Mmabatho was already talking to them as if they had been our friends for years.

Andrea and Jean came from Brussels where, some years earlier, Mmabatho's mother had been deployed as the South African ambassador to Belgium. Mmabatho had lived in Brussels on and off for five years, studied at Antwerp University and was highly competent in French. I guess that was the reason she clicked with Andrea and Jean.

While Mmabatho had no problem talking to her new friends, the language barrier meant that communication was difficult for me and I felt uncomfortable sitting next to Jean in the seats behind our wives. From our brief interactions I had gathered that Andrea and Jean had arrived at the Kruger National Park the day before us. The bush camp we were staying at had been recommended to Andrea by her parents, who had been on holiday in South Africa recently. Jean had also told me in his broken English that they were leaving for Cape Town the following day.

Having agreed on which way the tracks were leading, Xoli and Nathi jumped back into the Land Rover and started the engine.

"Her trail is still pointing this way," said Xoli, carefully steering the Land Rover off the track and into the bush, "and her droppings are fresh."

"You mean the leopard?" asked Andrea.

"Yes. She must be somewhere nearby, perhaps even watching us."

As we negotiated our way forward, Xoli driving by feel, I chased the flies off my sweaty face. Because the Land Rover had been customised for tourists, it had no roof. We only had the khaki caps, which we had been given upon our arrival, to protect us from the scorching sun. It was unbearable.

A clearing appeared in front of us with a giant marula tree at its centre. It had been uprooted and the bark from its trunk peeled off. Next to the fallen tree were fresh mounds of elephant dung.

"The elephants did this." Xoli pointed at the fallen tree. "They wanted to get the marula fruit."

Xoli drove the Land Rover into the clearing, looking down at the earth as he did so. Finally he stopped, climbed out of the vehicle and called on Nathi to do the same. They both squatted and examined the ground next to the tyre on the driver's side.

"These are her cub's prints," Xoli said, standing and pointing excitedly at the ground, the wide gap between his front teeth showing. "She was heavily pregnant when we last saw her, some two months ago. The belly was big." He made a gesture with his hands over his own belly to show us all just how pregnant the leopard had been.

"Wow! How beautiful! I wish we could see her and her cub," Mmabatho said, turning to face me.

From the back seat Jean instinctively dropped his hands onto his wife's shoulders and squeezed them. Andrea turned her head and kissed his left hand lightly.

"Okay, guys, but I think we need to take a break first," said Xoli, opening a cooler box that he had taken from somewhere at the back of the Land Rover. "We have been going for a while now. We can carry on in a bit."

Before we had left the lodge Xoli had asked us what we would like him to bring along for an afternoon drink in the bush. We had unanimously voted for champagne. With help from Nathi, Xoli set up a small table and filled four glasses with champagne. There was also some biltong, peanuts and dried fruit.

Thirty minutes later we were off again. I had thought that the champagne would make the two ladies sleepy and we would then be able to head back to the sanctuary of the bar at our lodge, but I was wrong. If anything, the champagne had given them new energy.

"They like hunting late in the afternoon," said Xoli, "so we are more likely to see her now that it's getting dark."

I was fed up with the whole adventure and, now that late afternoon was turning into early evening, I was sure that we wouldn't get to see the leopard. But at that very moment the radio crackled to life – it was one of the rangers from the other Land Rovers. He spat out some Shangaan and Nathi spat some more Shangaan back at him. He didn't tell us what was going on, but Xoli quickly turned the Land Rover around and began driving back towards the lodge, picking up speed all the time.

About eight hundred metres from the lodge gates, we saw a leopard walking lazily along the road. Cameras were clicking as happy tourists busied themselves taking the pictures.

"She is cute, isn't she?" said Andrea as she stood up to take a picture.

"Please sit down. We don't want to provoke him," warned Nathi, the tracker.

Andrea shrugged disappointedly, sitting down as Nathi began to explain to us that the leopard was about two and half years old, and that he had been kicked out by his pregnant mother a few months earlier. He also told us that wherever the mother was at that moment, she probably had the cub. I watched Andrea clench her teeth into a huge smile as she took picture after picture of the swaggering leopard.

"And now we have seen all of the Big Five, we must celebrate!" I said, touching my wife's shoulder. "Not so, babes?"

"They came to the African wilderness to see the Big Five and they saw them all in one day," said Mmabatho. "Of course we must celebrate!"

The leopard slunk into the sanctuary of the bush, but the whirl of excitement lingered around us as Xoli drove us back to the lodge.

That evening the chef produced yet another amazing buffet – impala loin with a marula and mustard sauce, a Moroccan lamb curry with salsa and poppadoms, grilled chicken and variety of salads and soups. At the dinner table, Andrea's cell phone kept ringing. Although I couldn't understand what she was saying, it seemed to me that every time she answered her phone she was narrating how she had seen all of the Big Five and how she was now a bush expert. As she talked she would pause at regular intervals to take sips from her glass of champagne.

After dinner we sat at the bar while Jean and I drank some Johnnie Walker Black.

"Guys, we will be back shortly. I need to buy some postcards and gifts for friends," said Andrea, sliding off her stool. Mmabatho followed her to the gift shop.

They came back about twenty minutes later. Andrea insisted that she wanted to put her gifts in the room and also e-mail a friend from her laptop. She promised that she would not take long. Nathi, who had just joined us for a drink, accompanied her back to her cabin, as was routine for guests moving about at night.

Five minutes later Nathi came back. He told us that Andrea was still working in her room and was going to call for him on the landline at the bar to come and pick her up as soon as she was done.

While we waited for Andrea, Nathi regaled us with stories about the poachers that came into the park, trapped rhinos and killed them for their horn. He told us that the poachers sold the rhino horn to Japan and China, so that people there could make an aphrodisiac out of it. According to him, rhinos take forty minutes or so to mate and the aphrodisiac is designed to make a human being last just as long.

About twenty minutes later Andrea still hadn't called the bar. Jean tried to call her on her cell phone, but she didn't answer. I could sense he was concerned, but he laughed off his anxiety, joking that Andrea had probably fallen asleep after all the driving in the bush earlier. However, only a few minutes later Jean bade us goodnight and left with Nathi without even finishing his drink.

We were still at the bar, Mmabatho showing me the gifts she had bought for our family, when the phone rang. I didn't hear what the barman said – I was too busy trying to add up all the money my wife had spent on useless gifts and contemplating how long it was going to take to pay off our credit cards – but when he put the phone down he looked terrified. At that moment I saw several rangers marching past us. They were armed with hunting rifles.

"What's going on?" I asked the barman.

"She..." He paused as though to choose his next words carefully. "The lady you were with just now has been attacked by a leopard and we have to close the bar."

"What? Andrea?"

We didn't wait for confirmation. Instead we followed the armed rangers and trackers between the glowing lanterns towards cabin number ten, where Jean and Andrea were lodging. There at the door, we spotted Jean. He was on his knees, crying. In front of him was a body covered with a white sheet. There was blood all over the place. Mmabatho's eyes widened and became watery as she shot an uneasy glance at the lifeless body on the ground. I wanted to touch Jean, say something to him, offer my condolences, but I didn't know how.

A few rangers were dispatched immediately to go and hunt the marauding leopard. Nathi told us that if things happened like they had on that night the animal involved had to be killed immediately as it was likely to repeat its behaviour and attack again.

Mmabatho and I were up all night long. We didn't even try to sleep. Instead we sat on the bed with the lights on and the sofa against the door, even though it was locked. When I went to the small fridge in the corner to fetch Mmabatho some water, she followed me as if she was afraid that I would desert her. Even when I went to the toilet, she followed me.

"Why, mara, huh?" she asked nervously while I was still on the toilet. "I mean, why her? She was so happy."

"I don't know, babes. Like they say, the duty of the married woman is to train her husband to be a widower."

"I can't bear this . . ." she said, her voice choking. "We have to go."

"We'll go tomorrow. We can't leave tonight, babes."

As dawn broke we heard the rangers that had been dispatched to hunt the leopard come back to the lodge. They had failed in their mission.

CATCHING THE SUN

Ngwako Maja, a well-known sculptor at the Mashishimale Village near Phalaborwa, sat down on a stone and leaned back against a mopani tree. The sun shone on his face through the leaves. He stretched his legs out comfortably as he carved a long wooden spoon using a sharp axe. He had almost completed the rough work, and just had to smooth the rough edges with sandpaper. About three days earlier, a lightning strike had uprooted the mulberry tree under which he normally sat. This had happened during the day, and had been accompanied by hail and thunder. The earth where the tree used to be was still stained purple from the juice of the fallen berries. His wife, Makoma, was sitting beside him. She was singing a Sepedi traditional song out of tune while using a fork to squeeze the juice out of some marula fruit. Two cocks were crowing a few metres away, while others fought over a hen. There was a rustle of leaves where they were fighting.

"The witches of this village," said Ngwako to his wife as he put down the axe and picked up the sandpaper, "they are not happy with what we have achieved."

"What do you mean, papa?"

"They killed my favourite shade," he said, referring to the mulberry tree. "I'm telling you it is an omen. Something terrible is going to happen. Lightning always strikes where it has struck before. I soon must get the healer to come and chase the evil spirits of lightning away."

"We must," said Makoma. "I'm still trying to make sense of the dream that I told you about yesterday. I dreamt of Mapula, your brother's daughter. Remember I told you that she was giving birth to a baby boy that came out already with upper teeth like a goat? All the midwives, including myself, ran away after seeing that baby."

"As you know, a baby that grows upper teeth first is a taboo according to our customs. Maybe it is an indication of something."

Ngwako began to sand the head of the wooden spoon. Suddenly his four dogs began to bark. He stretched his neck out, but saw nothing. He had many orders today – ten wooden spoons – and had made only six so far. His wares were popular, and he had many customers. Some came from nearby villages. Some were white Afrikaners from Phalaborwa. Some customers came from as far away as Polokwane, Pretoria and Johannesburg; others came from the unknown countries beyond the salty waters. Almost everyone who visited the Kruger National Park lodges in Phalaborwa knew about him. He was the one who had made the most admired sculpture: a life-size figure of a man leaning over a lion that he had killed with his bare hands. The figure attracted many tourists to stay at the Hans Merensky Lodge.

The mopani tree had the horns of a cow nailed to its trunk. The cow had been slaughtered about three years earlier on the day their daughter, Mpho, completed her womanhood initiation ritual.

Flies buzzed around Makoma's face as she went on squeezing the juice out of the ripe marula fruit. She let the juice drip for several seconds into a yellow twenty-five-litre container before picking up the next fruit. On the floor lay the yellow marula peel and the seeds. The peel would be given to the goats, cattle and sheep as feed. Mohale, their thirteen-year-old son, was busy collecting the peel to put into the animals' kraal. The seeds would be left to dry in the sun for several weeks until they became hard as pebbles. After that a rock would be used to crush them so that a soft peanut-like substance could be removed. This was used as a food supplement. It tasted like groundnuts, and was used for the same purpose.

The marula juice played a major role in the community. After three days or so, it fermented into a powerful beer. Most people in the village believed that the beer was a cure for impotence. After drinking it, a man became an animal in bed, and most village women became pregnant around that time. For others in the village, marula beer was a good remedy for constipation. Some used marula beer for bad things like poisoning or bewitching their enemies. There were several stories of people being killed at marula beer-drinking sessions. This is so because it is the only beer that is not sold in the village. All you do is to simply invite friends and relatives to come and enjoy it with you as a token of friendship. The marula tree itself was important also for producing mopani worms, which were a great delicacy in the village. But the marula fruit is also loved by the mosquitoes, and that is why there were several cases of malaria in the village.

Makoma's youngest daughter, Neo, was watching her mother closely and she slapped away the flies while eating a marula fruit. She was also throwing a ripe marula fruit up in the air and catching it in her cupped hands. A column of red ants made their way in and out of the small hole next to the yellow container. Some were carting away a small fly that Neo had swatted a few minutes ago.

As Mohale took another bowl full of marula peel to the kraal, a car stopped in front of their gate. This was not unusual. Ngwako's customers visited him almost every second day to place orders for woodwork. Some people ordered in bulk and sold them in urban areas at marked-up prices.

The four dogs started barking and the chickens scurried for cover when the car stopped. It was a black Toyota RunX with Eastern Cape registration. Ngwako stood up. He was still holding the unfinished wooden spoon. A lizard that was clambering up the tree trunk towards the cow horns fell with a heavy thud. One of the dogs, Bova, was already chewing at the rear wheel of the car. The visitors were still inside, afraid to come out.

"Voetsek wena Bova!" Ngwako cursed at the dog and pointed for it to go away. "Tsamaya!"

The dogs slunk off towards the marula tree in the middle of the large cattle kraal, where they slumped down, panting lightly. Near the cattle kraal was a smaller kraal, which was for the goats and sheep. On the other side, next to the pig sty, was a pit toilet.

A short, stocky man on the passenger side was the first to come out. He was followed from the back by a short, light-skinned elderly woman, and then by the man who was driving. The woman protected herself from the scorching sun with a yellow umbrella. Ngwako watched them with curious eyes.

"Dumelang," the short, stocky man greeted him, speaking what sounded like halting Sepedi.

"Thobela!" responded Ngwako. "Lekae."

"Siphilile akukhonto!" the man responded.

As the man spoke, Ngwako noticed the gap between his front teeth. It also seemed to Ngwako that the greeting was the only Sepedi words the man knew. As Ngwako continued the conversation in Sepedi, the man switched to isiXhosa. Ngwako looked at his visitors without recognition. He looked at the driver, who was already fanning himself with a brown Dobbs hat. The dogs barked insistently from the kraal. One of them trotted back and forth with flattened ears while barking threateningly, mechanically and without stopping. Ngwako picked up a stone and threw it at the dog. The stone landed just in front of the dog, scaring it away. It immediately dropped its tail and ran towards the cattle kraal again. The barking stopped.

"Age, bo ntate. Are tseneng," said Ngwako as he pointed towards the house.

The man with the Dobbs hat had beads of perspiration trembling on his forehead. He wiped his brow with the back of his hand.

"We are not sure if we are at the right place, but we are looking for the Maja family," the man said uneasily, mixing English and isiXhosa in one sentence. He had a bald head and grey whiskers.

"You are not lost. You may come in."

Ngwako led them to his five-bedroom house, built of red facebrick. He pushed open the front door and ushered the guests to the maroon sofas in the lounge. After the greeting formalities, the three visitors introduced themselves. The man with the Dobbs hat did the introductions. He was Sisanda Mbekeni. He introduced the woman as Amanda, who was married to the Mkefa family.

The short, stocky man was Xolani Voko. The woman was the sister to Zama Mondi and aunt to Meli, and they all hailed from Dutywa, Mbewuleni, in the Eastern Cape.

Makoma came in for the greetings and then went to the kitchen to prepare drinks for the visitors, as she usually did. She cast anxious glances from the kitchen as she removed the cold 1.5-litre Coke bottle from the refrigerator.

"As you see us here we are the messengers of bad news," the stocky man began. "Shame has befallen us. We have been asked by the Mondi family to come and announce the passing away of our beloved daughter, who is your biological daughter Mpho."

Ngwako looked at the man for a long minute without a word. His hands were resting on his thighs. He removed them and scratched his head with the tips of his fingers as if summoning the right words.

"You are not making any sense," he said with confusion. "You mean you drove all the way from the Eastern Cape to come tell me this?"

"There has been an accident, baba, and your daughter Mpho was unlucky. She died on her way to the hospital."

Ngwako stared at them silently, without blinking. He sat meditating after these words were spoken. He remained perfectly still, and did not even fall back in his chair. In the kitchen, Makoma sobbed, her voice muffled by the thick folds of a tea towel.

"And where was that?" he asked in a pitiful voice.

"Between Mthatha and Dutywa," the woman answered mournfully. "Apparently the car that they were driving tumbled down the cliff and rolled several times." She paused. "It hit the boulder, bounced off, and Mpho came out through the window. I think she didn't have her seatbelt on."

"What was she doing there?" Ngwako asked with a perplexed look. There was gentle sorrow in the lines that had developed across his forehead. "Her home is here in Phalaborwa, and we do not have relatives ko mathoseng."

"Well, they were coming to show us the newborn baby with her man who is our son, Meli."

Ngwako was startled. He looked closely at the woman, his dislike of her growing. Then he clasped his arms around his knees as he tried hard to understand what she was saying to him. He kept quiet for a while as if listening to his heart thump. Then his nostrils suddenly flared and his eyes snapped.

"What are you saying?" He stood up as if to go to the kitchen, but decided against it. "So, our daughter was staying with your son? MaMpho!" he called to his wife. "Did you know about this? My daughter is dead? She was living with a man. She was pregnant. She had a child. She had an accident? Actually, what are you telling me? How come I don't know about all these things?"

There was no answer from the kitchen. Instead there was the sound of glasses shattering on the tiled floor, accompanied by weeping and broken sobs. Makoma was shaking, and she held her stomach with both hands. She let out a piercing cry that seemed to ring in the ears long after it had ceased.

"Stop that and answer me, woman!" he demanded. For an instant he placed his hands over his ears. "Did you know all along that she was pregnant and living with a man? I heard you speaking to her the day before yesterday on the phone."

She did not answer. Defeated, Ngwako went back and sat silently on the sofa, his face looking down. He gazed at the calendar on the wall as if mulling over the dates. From the kitchen, Makoma yelled again, casting up her tear-filled eyes.

"I swear on the skeleton and spirit of my grandmother who lies below the earth in Ga-Kgapane! Whoever killed my daughter will eat her raw," she shouted between sobs. "The person will see a snake's buttocks! They will point where the snake has urinated!"

"It is very unfortunate that this happened," the woman visitor said hesitantly as Makoma's wailing subsided. "It was the will of God! My brother Zama, who is Meli's father, is also heartbroken. That is why he has sent us here to come and break the sad news and also to negotiate with the Maja family about how to go about the burial arrangements. The Mondi family wants to help in this regard."

For Ngwako, the words felt as if something swollen and painful had suddenly burst inside his heart. The woman looked at him steadily while turning a silver bracelet round and round on her left wrist. Makoma was standing at the kitchen door, her eyes alive with hatred for the visitors and aglow with the feverish terror of what had happened to her family.

"Iyo nna mawe! Mathosa abulayile nwanake!" She stamped her feet on the tiles. "These Xhosa witches have killed my educated daughter. They want to use her blood to make themselves rich! Not my daughter! You'll have to eat her raw!"

Ngwako took some time to master his confusion. He stood up, took a step forward, as if going to the kitchen, and then tightened his jaw.

"What can we do?" the stocky man tried to comfort him. "It was the will of God."

"God has no business in this!" shouted Makoma from the kitchen. "You Xhosas killed my daughter! Why did you kill her, huh? Why? She was too young to die. You should have killed me instead. I should not be burying my daughter at this young age. She was only twenty-three. She is the one who is supposed to be burying us, her parents. I'm still too young to mourn my daughter, you hear me? You must leave now!"

"Well, I don't think I can handle this alone," said Ngwako, his eyes flashing fiercely. "I'll send the child over to call my brother. His compound is not far from here."

Mohale was sent to tell his uncle Kagisho that he must come immediately. Meanwhile the curses poured from the kitchen.

"Whoever killed my daughter will have to eat her raw!" Makoma repeated, with virulent anger. "Otherwise the person will see the snake's buttocks!"

She burst into hysterical weeping. Ngwako leaned over and covered his eyes in a spasm of despair. His chest began to heave with suppressed emotion.

"Shut up, MaMpho!" commanded Ngwako. "You are devious! All along you knew and never told me? What kind of a wife are you?"

"We are very sorry for this," said the stocky man introduced as Xolani Voko. It was as if he was personally responsible. "Nowadays kids do things that have bad consequences."

Ngwako opened his mouth wide, as if in awe, and then closed it again. He let the sweat drip down his face for a while. Then he tried to control himself and bit his lower lip for few seconds.

"So, where is this son of yours who has impregnated and killed my daughter?"

"He is lying critical at the hospital in Mthatha."

"So, he survived and my daughter died?" Ngwako's voice trembled as he said the words, and he almost broke down.

"Well, he did survive with the child."

"My God! Who was driving?"

"As far as we were told, Meli was driving. Mpho was sitting in the passenger seat and the baby was strapped in her child seat at the back. She survived."

"So, where is my daughter's body now?" He struggled for composure, and tears filled his eyes.

"She is in the mortuary in Dutywa," said the woman. "We have decided to come here first before we could send her."

"So how long were the two together?" Ngwako asked.

"We heard they were together for over a year now. They were studying at the same university in Johannesburg, but our son was a senior. About six months ago our son started work at some firm called KPMG in Johannesburg. They were planning to get married in a few months, and it was the second time that he had brought her home."

"So, you never bothered to come and tell us about the pregnancy?"

"We were waiting for him to give us an indication. Unfortunately he travelled overseas for some training and only came back a few days after the baby was born." She choked, as if the words were burning her throat. "When the accident happened he was on his way home to make such arrangements."

At that moment Makoma sounded like she had been seized by a sudden attack of asthma. She was already soaked in sweat from the suffocating heat in the kitchen. Meanwhile, Mohale arrived with Kagisho, whose bald head glistened with perspiration. Ngwako was surprised that his brother had come so quickly. He didn't expect him at that moment, since he walked slowly, as if he had a bloated scrotum. Kagisho was immediately briefed about the sad news. Then there was silence for a while, and he began very slowly, as if groping for words. As he talked, foam appeared at the corners of his mouth.

"Well, as far as we, the Maja family, are concerned," began Kagisho after clearing his throat, "our daughter is still alive at the University of Johannesburg." He paused and looked at the visitors, one after the other. His eyes had an extraordinary power of penetration. "We sent her to the University of Johannesburg to study, and not to get a husband, a baby, or die. We sent her to get a degree. As far as we are concerned she is doing her third year in Commerce, and not lying in a cold fridge somewhere ko mathoseng. If she is pregnant, or was pregnant, or there is any suitor, we are expecting that family to come and discuss her marriage with us. We will be waiting."

The man with the Dobbs hat was listening open-mouthed. It was obvious that the visitors were taken by surprise. Ngwako covered his eyes with his hand.

"But she has already died. We have to think of ways of burying her soon." There was a flash of impatience in the Dobbs man's eyes as he spoke. "We have to come to that agreement soon because the more she stays in the mortuary, the more expensive it will be."

Kagisho shook his head slowly. His lips were moist with spittle. He didn't answer promptly. Instead he looked at the man for several seconds.

"Like we said before, we cannot mention mortuary in this house. Our daughter is not dead, and she does not know a man." There was no trace of bitterness in Kagisho's voice. "No man came to ask our hand yet for us to give him permission to spoil her. If you are interested we can talk about marriage because, as far as we know, our beautiful daughter is alive. We know this because we are the ones that brought her onto this earth. We look after her, both morally and financially, and that is why we sent her to the University in Johannesburg, and not to some mortuary in the Eastern Cape."

"This is not working. It is not what we hoped for," said the stocky man, clearly shocked. "What we will do is we will transfer her body to the nearest mortuary here in Phalaborwa. We will pay for all the expenses, including the arrangement of her burial."

The words were said so seriously and so bluntly that Kagisho and Ngwako could not respond immediately. Kagisho straightened his back before looking at the man. It was obvious that his bubble of calm had been pricked.

"Well, maybe that is a proper way of doing things in your Xhosa tradition," said Kagisho, rubbing his hands. "But we are the Bapedi. We have to communicate with her spirit and the ancestors first."

"But time is running out." The stocky man's manner was careless and almost insolent.

"Your time, not ours."

"So, what do we do now?"

"I think we have already told you what to do," Kagisho answered curtly. "You will have to marry our daughter first."

"Marry her?" Amanda said with shock. "How do you marry a dead person?"

"We must negotiate lobola first, because she's not dead, according to us," said Kagisho with finality.

"Unbelievable! That is both ridiculous and unreasonable," said the stocky man, with an exclamation of impatience. "As we suggested, we will transfer the body to the nearest Phalaborwa mortuary. We will let you know which one."

Kagisho looked at the man, obviously baffled at the absurdity of his words. His immediate response was a shrug of his shoulders before shaking his head vehemently. Then he started talking, with his voice rising gradually and expressing his distaste. At that point Ngwako's head was lowered between his knees. Raising his terror-stricken face, Ngwako saw that his brother's eyes were also full of tears.

"Ulibambe lingashon' ilanga!" said Kagisho with rage. "You hear me?" He wagged his right finger vigorously. "You must catch the sun, and hold it close to your chest, for it must not set for you! Ulibambe!"

A moment of profound silence followed. Then Kagisho bent his head towards Amanda and repeated the words.

"Ulibambe lingashon' ilanga!"

"Well, we are God-fearing people," said Amanda dismissively. "We are born-again Christians."

"How dare you impregnate our daughter and only tell us when she is already dead. I have never seen anyone who behaves like you do in my life," said Kagisho, looking Amanda straight in the face while trying to meet her eyes. "When our daughter is already in the mortuary, dead, you Xhosas have the nerve to come here and tell us about her death. Why didn't you come immediately when you realised that she was pregnant? Is this how you do things in Xhosa culture?"

It was evident that there was no hope of settling the argument between the two families. The visitors stood up. Their parting was bitter. In the kitchen, Makoma's face flushed angrily, and she looked as if she might attack someone with her hands. She watched as the visitors left the house, and the man pushed his Dobbs hat onto his head. All she could do was to bow her head in her hands with a sob of pain. The whole meeting now sounded like an abandoned fight.

As soon as they were gone, Makoma went to her room and wept. It was an inconsolable weeping that lasted for several weeks. She could not sleep at night. She thought about her daughter every day, and her eyes were moist from crying so much. She would get up in the middle of the night weeping with pain and fury. She did not eat for a couple of days, but she vomited the whole night. When she started talking to herself, Kagisho advised his brother that it was dangerous having her around. The discovery of a dead cat in the compound was taken as a premonition. Someone in the village was bewitching them and they had to do something before it was too late. According to Kagisho, someone jealous had done this and the family had to do some cleansing.

Three days and nights slid along with difficulty for the Maja family as the clouds of despair enveloped them. Every day there were tears. The circle of empathisers began to increase. Men and women from the village arrived at the household every day, one by one, to offer their condolences after they heard the sad news. The women cried openly, and the men sobbed secretly.

On the fourth day they received a call from the Phalaborwa mortuary. The body of their daughter had arrived, and they were told that the Mondis had paid until the coming Friday. But the Majas never went to the mortuary.

A week passed, and time put things in their place. In the Eastern Cape, Amanda was struck by lightning on her way home to Butterworth. She died on the spot. Before Amanda had even been buried, Zama's daughter, Nombu, who was studying at the Walter Sisulu University of Technology, was attacked by her boyfriend's lover, who poured acid on her face. Nombu was now in hospital needing surgery for severe burns. The Mondi family suspected that the Pedis had killed Amanda with the lightning in retaliation for their daughter's death. Zama had received the news while in his shop in Mbewuleni with his aunt, Nozi.

"All this bad luck is happening because of the Maja spell." That was all Zama could say to his aunt, and he looked deeply affected by the loss to his family.

"How did this happen to Nombu?" asked Nozi, a crack of anger in her voice.

"Apparently the lady who did this to her was dressed up in a veil and followed her along Kruger Street," replied Zama, with tears in his eyes. "She then threw the acid in my daughter's face."

"How bad is she?" his aunt asked in a concerned tone.

"They say she has suffered burns on her face, neck and chest.

Now I have two of my own children in the hospital and my own sister at the mortuary."

The Mondi family decided that enough was enough. Zama, who was a well-respected businessman in Mbewuleni, decided that they should drive to Phalaborwa to sort things out with the Maja family. That Wednesday, he bravely telephoned the Majas after getting the contacts from the mortuary staff. He arranged to come and see them for further negotiations on Saturday morning.

On Friday afternoon Zama and his people booked into the Hans Merensky Lodge. That night, he received a call from the hospital saying that Meli had succumbed to his injuries. Zama was a devastated man, and looked like he had aged in just a few days.

On Saturday morning, the Mondi family arrived at the Majas' compound. The dogs announced the visitors by making whining noises, their tails tucked between their legs and ears flattened. They retreated and sat under the mopani tree when Ngwako silenced them. Mohale and his younger sister, Neo, were there, together with an older girl of about eighteen years. Her name was Shoki, and she was Kagisho's daughter. She had shapely breasts that threatened to burst out of her blue blouse. Neo was sucking her thumb, and observed the visitors with large and startled round eyes as they were ushered into the dining room. She didn't give any sign of understanding what was going on or what was said, but looked terrified and curious. Silently, she looked at them with a long and hateful eye. She knew them from their previous visit, and was aware that they had caused her mother great pain.

Mohale was busy plucking a chicken that had just been slaughtered to feed the guests. Makoma was not there. The family had decided to send her to her mother's place in Ga-Kgapane to try and ease the bitter weight of suffering. In her place was Kagisho's wife, Mapula.

Zama had done some research into Bapedi marriage arrangements by talking to some of the workers at the Hans Merensky Lodge. Before he entered through the gate, he took out of the car a crate of twelve 1.5-litre cool drink bottles and a bottle of Richelieu brandy for the Majas. Kagisho asked Shoki to take the crate of drinks inside the house while he welcomed the Mondis. Since the morning she had been busy preparing food in the roofless outside kitchen. The Maja family had also bought a separate crate of cool drinks for the guests.

Concealing his dislike, Kagisho put out a broad, flat hand to welcome Zama, before ushering the guests into the house. The visitors wiped imagined sand off the soles of their shoes before they entered the dining room. Zama scanned the room. Mapula and another woman named maMatete were sitting on a grass mat spread on the floor in the corner, not far from the sofas. Mapula's complexion was light, suggesting the use of skin-lightening cream. maMatete was an elderly woman in her mid-sixties, and her hair was tinged with grey. She was pushing huge pinches of snuff up each nostril when they entered. She sat up and blew her nose before wiping away the grains of snuff with the back of her hand.

Nozi joined the women on the grass mat, and the men sat on the sofas. Behind the three women, Zama noticed a newly carved figurine of a mother sitting cross-legged, a child lying in her lap. He was fascinated. On her head the figurine wore a doek, and her head was slightly raised and her mouth open, revealing filed teeth.

The baby's head was tilted towards its mother's left breast. Zama squatted and touched the figurine for a few seconds before joining Ntate Lefifi and Ntate Maake on the sofa. Both were relatives of the Maja family. Shoki came in with two unopened 1.5-litre bottles of Coke and Sprite. She also brought a tray with eight floral glasses for the guests to serve themselves.

After the introductory formalities, Nozi coughed to break the awkward silence. It all sounded strange to Zama as his aunt talked.

"We are here as the Mondi family again," she began, with an effort. "We know that in our previous meeting things didn't come out as we had desired. We apologise on our side for whatever inconveniences we may have caused. We hope we are forgiven and that the bad luck that has befallen our family since then may stop immediately."

"I'm glad you didn't come with those disrespectful people," Kagisho chimed in, softened by the tone of the apology.

"Again, we are sorry about what happened the last time," she said, clasping her veinous and knotted hands together. "We are here today not to fight with the Maja family, but to ask forgiveness for what our son has caused in your family. We also came to make peace and build a relationship with this family. Although our daughter has passed away and is not buried yet, we would like to take this opportunity to do things the proper traditional way by negotiating for her lobola first." She paused and looked around for any sign of objection.

No one spoke. MaMatete took out her snuffbox again. She opened it with trembling hands, and spilt half of it on the floor. It was then that Zama remembered to take some money out of his pocket. It was not the lobola money, but to make the Maja family open their mouths to speak in the negotiation process. Otherwise they would not talk.

Zama put the two thousand rands on the table. There was silence as Ntate Lefifi took the money and counted it, without a word. Everyone looked at him as he wetted his thick fingers at each loud count. His bald head gleamed as though it was coated with Vaseline. They all sat perfectly still, listening and watching as he counted. His eyes were half-shut. When he finished counting he looked at Ngwako, Ntate Maake and Kagisho, who all nodded. MaMatete looked on quietly with her snuffbox in her hand. Then she took another gentle pinch of snuff and seasoned the floor with it while murmuring something to the invincible ancestors.

"Realeboga. Thank you!" she said, looking at Zama and his aunt. "Now the negotiations may start."

Zama was anxious to get this over and done with so that he could concentrate on the death in his family.

"Thank you," said Zama, drawing in his breath with an exaggerated show of patience.

"We would like to know how much it will cost us to extend our relations with the Maja family by asking your daughter Mpho to be part of the Mondi family in marriage," Zama's aunt said as she watched little clouds of snuff dribbling through MaMatete's fingers over the front of her dress.

"Well, as you know how we fought in the previous meeting, we were not expecting this kind of cordiality from your side," Ntate Lefifi started as he watched MaMatete shake the snuff from her fingers. "However, we are willing to negotiate with you. If you give us a few minutes to discuss this, we will come back to you with an answer."

The representatives of the Maja family left the house and went outside. They entered a separate thatched hut that was not attached to the big house. Thirty minutes passed while they discussed the proposal. Meanwhile, inside the main house, the Mondi family waited and grew impatient. After forty minutes, the Maja family sent MaMatete with their reply.

"The Maja family wants thirty cows or thirty-five thousand rands for the marriage. We also want two three-piece suits for the fathers of the bride." She paused, raised a trembling hand to pinch her nose, and then continued. "The suits must be black, size thirty-six and thirty-eight, and must be double-breasted."

"What?" asked Zama, nostrils flaring and eyes snapping.

"It is as I say to you," she insisted.

"Tell them that we cannot afford it. We have also been plagued by bad luck in our family. The bridegroom, my son Meli, has also passed away this morning. We also lost my sister Amanda, who was here in the previous failed negotiation, through lightning." There was fear and worry on his face and in the tone of his voice. "My daughter Nombu is in serious pain at the hospital as we speak, after acid was poured on her face. We're not sure if she will survive. Tell them that we still have to bury our son and his aunt and pay medical expenses for our daughter. We can only afford ten thousand. And we will cover your daughter's stay in the mortuary as well as her burial."

MaMatete stood up and went to the thatched hut with the message. By that time Shoki had finished the cooking, and she came to the hut to ask whether she should dish up for the visitors. Ntate Maake instructed her not to as they were still busy negotiating. The family had a little caucus for about fifteen minutes before sending MaMatete out again.

"We the Maja say that this is the fair amount that you must pay. We understand your sorrows, but we have ours too." She paused and looked at Zama. "We say that our daughter was a virgin when she met your son. We worked so hard sending her to an expensive university in Johannesburg. She is going to qualify and have a good job, as this is her final year at the university according to us. When she graduates she will help her siblings to also succeed in life through education. But since your son has chosen her for eternal life, there is nothing we can do. Like they say, love conquers everything. We will only allow her to join the Mondi family if you are prepared to compensate us with the amount we have asked of you. This is not by any means selling our daughter to you. We are trying to build a relationship according to our daughter's wish, as she has chosen your family. We assume it was her wish because she ended up being pregnant and having a child with your son."

Zama and his aunt shook their heads in unison. No one said a word, as they had agreed on the way to the compound not to offend the Maja family. But it was obvious that Zama was fretting.

"Okay," he said finally, anger visible in his eyes. "Give us a moment to discuss it with my aunt and we will get back to you in the next five minutes."

Meanwhile, the Maja family agreed to dish up the food for the visitors after MaMatete had pleaded that they looked hungry.

Mapula was given the responsibility of taking a pot of chicken and rice to the visitors, which she did with the help of her daughter Shoki. Before they could eat, Zama sent Aunt Nozi to the hut to relay the message. She found them eating, as Shoki had dished out the other chicken, which was served in a separate pot.

"The Mondis are begging that you please reduce the bride price. We agree with everything that you have just said, but it is too steep for the family," she pleaded with concentrated effort. "May we agree on twenty cows at least since we both lost our loved ones, and we won't have the benefit of our makoti since she has passed away."

Kagisho's face froze at the mention of death, deepening into a frown of dislike and distrust. Ntate Maake told the aunt that they would send MaMatete after they had eaten.

The sun had gone halfway across the afternoon sky when the Maja family sent MaMatete with word that the offer for the bride was final and non-negotiable.

"Our daughter is a good virtuous woman who has been initiated in all the tribe's ways. According to us she has known no man."

A flurry of anger ran through Zama again. He could tell that the Majas were not willing to compromise on the lobola price. After MaMatete had left them alone, he had a brief moment with his aunt before he sent her again to the Majas.

"With your permission, we the Mondis are asking to sleep on this matter. We would like to come back tomorrow morning to conclude our negotiations."

* * *

The Mondis arrived just as one of the male dogs had mounted the bitch at the cattle kraal. Mohale threw a stone at the dogs, but it hit the pole of the kraal, and was just enough to scare them. The dogs ran off, but the male's penis was stuck inside the bitch. Neo sat under the mopani tree and sucked in the snot that ran from her nostrils. With the back of her hand, she wiped away the tears that ran down her face. She was obviously still mourning the loss of her sister.

Both families were represented by the same people as the previous day. It was the same arrangement, with the Majas in the hut and the Mondis inside the big house. Zama and his aunt paid the thirty-five thousand rands in cash and brought the two suits. Aunt Nozi carried the money in a black briefcase and the suits on nice suit hangers. She also gave them the receipts for the two suits in case they didn't fit. The suits had been bought at Markham in Phalaborwa.

"What about the child?" asked Kagisho after Ntate Lefifi had counted the money in front of everyone present inside the hut. "You must pay her lobola too."

After back-and-forth negotiations, they came to an agreement of ten thousand for the three-month-old girl. The families agreed that the Mondis would hire a nanny to look after her. They also agreed that she should visit the Majas at least every December in Mashishimale. The girl's name was Botho.

That Saturday, Mpho was buried in the cemetery in Mashishimale Village. The Mondis didn't attend, and understandably so. They were also burying their dead. But they contributed ten thousand towards her funeral.

MY NAME IS PEACHES

I have come to say goodbye to you, Tshif. Do you still remember me?

Let me remind you. We first met at Shivava, in Newtown, downtown Jozi. Just like you, the place no longer exists, but this was back sometime in August 2004. You were our loyal customer and I was your beautiful waitress. At least, that is what you always used to say. Without fail, at four in the afternoon every Friday you came to eat at Shivava. And every Friday it was the same, your favourite, pap and mopani worms. Ag, sies! Those things! You said they were delicious and nutritious. I was not convinced. When I served them to you the first time, I thought those creatures would come alive again in your stomach and that you would die slowly as they ate through your gut. But you survived, and the next Friday you were back again for another plate of pap and mopani worms.

Now that you and I are history, let me put the record straight. The only reason I looked forward to serving you and your friend Matome in those early days was that you always left me a good tip. Yes, you did. One of my friends at the restaurant advised me that people like you, who came to eat, tipped better than people who came only to drink. And in your case, Tshif, she was right.

I knew what you liked, Tshif. You would start your Friday with a double tot of Jameson. When you said "two fingers on the rocks", I knew what you meant. But as the afternoon turned into the evening, you changed to Windhoek Lager. That was you, Tshif.

You worked for Spoornet as a goods train driver. You told me even before I asked that you lived in Winchester Hills, a posh suburb. I informed you that I stayed in Hillbrow's Mariston student accommodation and that I was a first year management student at Rosebank College in Braamfontein. Like I told you then, the reason I worked as a waitress was to augment what my parents gave me every month. Johannesburg can be very expensive for a girl.

Then, one special Friday evening, after my shift, instead of taking my usual delivery taxi, you insisted on dropping me at Mariston. You were with your friend Matome, who was also your colleague. Though I hesitated, I was happy to save the ten rand I would have spent on the delivery taxi. I still remember the song that began to play when you started your car: "Four Women" by Nina Simone. That is where my name – Peaches – comes from.

As you dropped me off, you shyly asked me out on a date the following day. I told you that I worked awkward shifts, and you didn't insist. I didn't know it then, but I was only playing hard to get.

On Saturday morning you came in at around ten for your breakfast. I was working until twelve and the end of my shift coincided with the end of your meal. You insisted on taking me to my place again. Only this time you were alone, and, as we drove along Bree Street, you asked me some questions about myself. All along you'd thought I was a Mosotho from Lesotho, so when I told you I was from Matatiele in East Griqualand, in the foothills of the Drakensberg, you were very surprised.

"I'm not a Mosotho. I'm a Phuthi," I told you.

You had never heard of my nation. You are not the only one, you know. Most South Africans don't know the Baphuthi. For them there are only Zulus, Xhosas and Sothos. You asked me to speak a sentence in isiPhuthi and I did. I no longer remember what I said, but you laughed. You confessed you had not heard the language before. In your ears, you said my language was like a strange combination of seSotho and isiZulu. I was not offended at all. Instead I started telling you the history of my nation. You sounded interested, unlike most other guys. Maybe that is what impressed me about you.

I told you that the Baphuthi came into being around the time of the Mfecane. Just like the Bhaca people, who ended up in the Eastern Cape, my ancestors were running away from the mighty sword of King Shaka's army. During this time they found refuge in the thick bush near the Drakensberg. As the advancing Zulu warriors neared the bush, the African duikers (phuthis) that were grazing there sprang out and ran away. The warriors went after the animals, as they needed fresh meat, and the people were saved. That is how we came to be called the Baphuthi, or the duikers.

We talked a lot that Saturday and I was beginning to like you. Then you asked if I would go with you and Matome to a soccer game at FNB Stadium later that afternoon. Chiefs and Pirates were playing at around four. How could a rural girl like me resist? Still, I was not yet entirely sure about you, which is why I suggested that I bring along my two friends who stayed with me at Mariston, Samu and Nolo.

When you came to fetch us with your friend, Matome, we were so excited. On our way to the stadium you asked us what we would like to drink and I told you that I didn't drink. The reason I told you this is that I didn't want you to think that we were gold diggers. Some men run away once they realise that a girl is expensive. But my friends saw an opportunity and asked for Red Square. We only ever drank Russian Bear vodka when we were together, it was the cheapest option for students like us, so it was nice to be able to ask for something more expensive. And I must say that I was happy when you insisted that I should also taste Red Square. You bought eighteen bottles of it at Columbine in Meredale by the mini Pick n Pay. We then went to Tinties in Naturena, by Sun City Prison, where we braaied lots of meat.

By the time you drove us to FNB Stadium, I was drunk and no longer wary of you. That is why I was not shy to ask you to find the nearest garage so that my friends and I could pee. It was then that you started to call me Peaches, instead of my real name.

At the stadium we stayed in the car drinking until our Red Square was finished. We were playing a song by Zola and singing happily. Remember:

> *Ngiyak'thanda ntombazane, no matter what they say.*
> *The way this thing is going sofa silahlane.*

What a song!

You guys still had your Windhoek Lagers in the cooler box. Samu joined you and drank two of those.

Fifteen minutes before the game started we lined up at Gate H, bottles in hand. Right at the gate, the security guards told us that we could not take alcohol inside. You and Matome finished your Windhoeks and threw the empty bottles in the rubbish bin. As you did this, one of the security guards told you that he sold cellulars. I didn't know what he meant, but then I saw you giving the guy fifty rand in exchange for two Bell's nip bottles. We hid them inside my handbag, remember? I asked why they were called cellular, and you told me it was because they were small like a cell phone.

My girls and I were very excited to be inside FNB Stadium for the very first time. Nolo came from Don Doni, or Dundonald, in Mpumalanga, as she told you. Samu came from Mahehle in Ixopo, KwaZulu-Natal. None of us had ever been in a stadium like that before.

We sat in the Pirates stand because that was the team you supported. You were wearing their beautiful black soccer jersey with *TSHIF 10* written on the back. My friends and I were not into soccer, but the atmosphere was great. Unfortunately, I didn't see most of the game as I was vomiting in the toilets for a whole hour. That is why I asked you for the car keys. I wanted to go and sit inside the car in the parking lot with Samu. She was happy to accompany me to the car because there were still cold Windhoeks in the cooler box and both cellulars were finished. Inside the car I drank lots of water with ice. By the time the game finished I was almost sober, but throwing up, or trumpeting, as you guys called it, had made me hungry. You suggested that we go to Soweto, to your favourite Karaoke Chicken Inn, somewhere in Diepkloof. After that you drove us to The Rock in Rockville, where DJ Sbu was playing, remember?

Oh, what a night! We had never been to Soweto before and it rocked. Nolo immediately joined the dance floor, Matome danced with Samu, but I preferred sitting with you.

You drove us back to your Winchester Hills apartment at about two in the morning. We were singing along with Thandiswa Mazwai:

Yindaba kabani uma ndilahl'umlenze!

That song was on repeat for the thirty minutes it took us to get back to your place.

We were supposed to sleep that morning, but we didn't. We continued drinking. But you spoiled our mood when you started playing strange white people's songs. We complained. We wanted some kwaito or house music, but you refused. Eventually, your choice of songs – "Iris" by the Goo Goo Dolls and "You're Beautiful" by James Blunt – lulled us to sleep on the sofa.

We woke up at about ten or eleven in the morning when you played "Four Women" by Nina Simone at a very high volume. It was on repeat, and you stood in the middle of the sitting room, in only your boxer shorts, shouting "My name is Peaches!" as if you were mad. That was funny. From that day on, you and I called each other Peaches. Partly, it was because you had forgotten my name that morning, as you later confessed. But you earned my trust because you and Matome never tried to take advantage of any of us when we were drunk. As you know, that is what most men do.

That Sunday morning you suggested that we order two full Nando's chickens instead of going to braai at Tinties again. Everyone agreed as we were all hungry and babalas. Meanwhile, Nolo was scanning your whisky collection. You had bottles of Hennessy, Johnnie Walker Blue, Jameson, Tullamore Dew, Chivas Regal, Glenmorangie and Glenfiddich. My friends and I were very impressed by your collection and before the Nando's arrived we were already drinking. I settled on the Hennessy, Samu on the Johnnie Walker Blue, that she called Johnnie motsamai, and Nolo on the Chivas. What we didn't know then was that you had simply filled the expensive bottles with cheap stuff. As you told me several years later, what we had thought was Hennessy, Johnnie Walker Blue and Chivas was actually concoctions of Klipdrift, Firstwatch and Bell's that you had simply poured into the empty bottles. Silly man!

We were joined by one of your friends, Sifiso, as we sat by the pool at your townhouse after eating. I remember Samu nearly drowned while trying to swim and it was Sifiso who helped her out. We had a great time at your place and that was the first night I slept with you. Nolo slept with Matome too, although she claimed afterwards that nothing had happened. Samu blacked out and did not remember a thing.

The following Monday you drove us back to Mariston and we called each other Peaches all the way.

The next time I visited you, I was alone. Remember that night? We were wild.

What went wrong between us, Tshif? Yes, I know that I made

the mistake of relating our bedroom adventures to my friends. Doesn't every woman make such mistakes? I was just excited. You know how girls like discussing silly stuff. While drinking Russian Bear in our res, I told the girls how you Venda boys are the most gifted down there. But is that a secret? After that, every time I spent the night with you, my friends always asked me about the things we did. I told them how adventurous you were, how you hated lame routines in bed. Nolo laughed very hard when I told them how I nearly broke my hip in Thokoza Park, under that willow tree. Remember, that's where you taught me that squat thing? At first it was very uncomfortable, it was like you were breaking my virginity all over again, but then you showed me the trick to it. And after that it was amazing, until I slipped and fell.

I thought Nolo and Samu were my best buddies and I trusted them. Maybe it was the Russian Bear that made me tell them. But it was also pride. Their adventures were not as exciting. Nolo talked about this ex of hers who'd had such a small penis that she called it "the mosquito". Samu confided in us that her man came very quickly.

Well, I had a different story to tell, and that is why from that day on my friends always asked about our adventures.

A month later, I was deeply hurt when I found out that you and that bitch Nolo had slept together. I felt betrayed by you and my so-called friend. Never mind, she is past tense now. But I won't forget that day.

I came to your apartment one Saturday night after my shift without telling you. I had begun to suspect that you might be seeing someone else because your behaviour towards me had changed.

You didn't open the door when I knocked, but I could hear music playing inside. It was "Four Women" by Nina Simone. I knew then that you were with a woman, but what I didn't know was that it was that bitch Nolo. I confronted you the following day and you denied it like Shaggy in that song "It Wasn't Me". You convinced me that you were out drinking somewhere with your friends that night and had just left your music playing in the apartment. Matome even gave you an alibi. I apologised, and even came to do your washing for you after that because I felt so guilty.

A month after that, Samu and Nolo fought over money and Samu confided in me that you and Nolo were seeing each other behind my back. She told me that your relationship with Nolo had started on the day that we had all gone round to your place for a braai. That afternoon I got drunk really quickly and passed out on your couch. You know what? Samu still thinks Nolo drugged me that day, lacing my Hennessy with brake fluid that they had bought together at Midas car spares. I think she's right. It makes sense when I look back at what happened. How else do you explain me sleeping for eleven hours straight? Tell me if I'm wrong, but I think she deliberately laced my drink so that you guys could have a good time together. But what about you, Tshif? I know she was dressed seductively – you claimed to have succumbed to temptation when I finally found out the truth – and perhaps I would have understood if it was only that once, but you guys slept together again and again. I still can't believe you both did that behind my back.

After that I refused to talk to you. My silence lasted for three months. Then your ass came crawling back, apologising profusely.

You even took me to the International Jazz Festival in Cape Town. That was my first time on a plane, the first time I saw the beautiful Republic of Cape Town, the first time I saw the ocean. It was in Cape Town that we started dating again, and things began to get serious. You had missed me; I had missed you too. You said you wanted me back, and I asked if you were serious after what had happened. You said yes. I asked if you were still seeing that bitch Nolo, and you said no. I believed you. I thought it was my fault that you two had started seeing each other behind my back because of the stories that I had told Nolo and Samu about us.

Another three months passed and things between you and me seemed back to normal. I had forgiven you. Then one day you told me that you had been offered a promotion, driving goods trains between Rustenburg and Mafikeng. You told me that if you took the job, you would be based in Mafikeng.

"What about us, Peaches?" I asked you, concerned.

"I'll be in Joburg every weekend, Peaches," you replied. "Mafikeng is just three hours' drive. I will make sure I visit you, and that you visit me every weekend."

We were drinking at Shivava when you told me all this, remember? I was no longer working there, but you still went there for your pap and mopani worms.

A week later you left for Mafikeng to start your new job. I was very sad because I was aware that long-distance relationships don't work. Do you remember how angry I was that morning? I had read one of the messages on your phone. It was from Nolo. She said that she was six months pregnant. I went outside to cry in the early hours of the morning. You thought I was sleepwalking. You didn't understand.

Today, as I reminisce, I'm here in Mafikeng. I only heard of your death yesterday. For the past three weeks we had not been on good terms. This was because I found out that you had sent your relatives to Nolo's home in Don Doni to acknowledge her child as your own. You told me on the phone that the child should not be made to suffer for the mistakes of the parents. You will understand why I didn't answer your calls or bother to reply to your messages after that.

Apparently you were in great agony when you died. Your female colleague, Sine, told us this in her eulogy. She was in pain, too, as she spoke. She said that you waited for help together and that during that time you called most of your friends and loved ones. She told the mourners that, because of the impact when the train derailed, your right leg was all but amputated. She said she did her best to staunch the bleeding, but you had lost a lot of blood by the time the helicopter arrived and you died on the way to hospital.

I first saw that I had twenty-two missed calls sometime around midday on Monday. The first one was at twelve twenty-seven am. The last one was at three forty-five am. Well, I was sleeping then. No, I'm lying. I was not sleeping. I was still at Sakhumzi, in Vilakazi Street in Orlando West. There was this super rich BEE guy there and he was charming Samu and me with a bottle of Hennessy. How could I answer your call? I knew you would have spoiled my fun. And anyway, I was still angry with you about that bitch Nolo.

Let me first tell you about this man. His name is Comrade Phila and he drives a brand new Range Rover Sport Supercharged, so new that it doesn't yet have number plates. Imagine if I had answered your call that night. You would have asked me where I was. And with that house music at Sakhumzi, you would have known I was still eating joy while you were in pain. The best thing was just to ignore your call. Anyway, I don't owe you an explanation. Not after what you did with that bitch Nolo.

I did try to return your calls on Tuesday morning, but your phone went straight to voicemail. Of course, you were already cold inside the government mortuary by then, but I did not know that.

It was Matome who finally told me the news. He called me yesterday morning, wanting to find out whether I would be at your funeral today. I was so shocked I nearly fainted. Matome had taken it for granted that I had also received the sad news on Monday morning.

Last night Samu and I were supposed to have dinner with Comrade Phila, but I gave him an excuse. I told him that I suspected I was pregnant. I had to be at your funeral, Peaches. Shame, the poor guy came to my apartment later and gave me flowers and two thousand rand to go and get an abortion. That is the money I used to come to your funeral.

I left Joburg alone at three thirty this morning. I didn't have time to get my hair and nails done. I didn't have time to shop for a new dress or shoes. All I could think about was driving to Mafikeng to bury my Peaches.

I nearly hit a donkey in Itsoseng. It was near the spot where we made love on our way back to Joburg from that Sixties party. You remember that night, Tshif? We pulled off the road and took advantage of the back seat of your Polo.

I was playing one of our favourite songs – Labi Siffre's "Something Inside So Strong" – when I passed Itsoseng. Remember how we played that song after making love again for the first time in Cape Town? I also played The Doves' "Beaten Up In Love Again", Lisa Fischer's "How Can I Ease the Pain", Boyz II Men's "End of the Road" and Simply Red's "Holding Back the Years". But it was Nina Simone's "Four Women" that I repeated over and over again until I arrived here in Mafikeng. The memories I have of you and that song will remain imprinted on my mind forever.

Before we buried you here this morning, I forced myself to look at your face one last time. Matome, who had seen your body at the mortuary, told me that you had been horribly injured in the accident, but you looked at peace inside the casket. Your body might have been damaged but your face was untouched – you were still handsome, even in death. I saw your dad blinking wearily as I turned away from the coffin, his eyes glassy with unshed tears. You once told me that he had been a musangwe champion, and I was convinced of it when I saw his clenched fists. It was as though he was fighting desperately for control of himself.

I didn't cry during the ceremony, Tshif. Maybe I am still in shock? I don't know. Luckily no one noticed my dry eyes because there were already several beautiful women crying by the time it all began. The one with the Brazilian weave was the loudest. She was pregnant, and kept muttering something in Setswana about her child being left fatherless. Your female colleague, who had been with you inside the train, was also inconsolable. She was very lucky – she had escaped with only a broken arm. I didn't notice her until she stood up to give her eulogy, just as I didn't notice the message written on the plaster that covered her arm until we were at the graveside: *Rest in peace, Peaches.*

Who else could she be referring to, Tshif?

Is she carrying your child, too?

Did you sleep with her, as well?

Today I feel deeply disappointed in you, Tshifhiwa Mafela. I feel betrayed. I came to your funeral thinking I was the only woman in your life, the only woman you loved, but there were at least four of us. When my friends warned me that you Venda boys rarely marry outside your tribe, I should have taken heed. Yes, that's right, your fiancée was at the funeral, too. Of course she was, Tshif! I was obviously surprised to learn that you were actually living with her in Mafikeng. What's her name again? Livhuwani? She was with your daughter, Mutondi, who is three years old. You never told me about either of them, but it is clear that, as far as your family are concerned, she is your wife, or widow.

I also didn't know that you had fathered three other children besides Mutondi and Nolo's baby. Their names were in the funeral programme. Let me ask you a question: Did you ever think about HIV when you slept with all of us without protection? I'm saying this because I found out this morning that I'm eight weeks pregnant with your child. You see, I wasn't lying when I told Phila yesterday that I was pregnant. It is just not his child – I'm sure of it. But now that you're gone it will be his. I'm not doing the abortion thing.

Wow! It's after midday now, and very hot here in Mafikeng. I loved you, Peaches, and even now, now that I know the truth, my feelings for you are still the same. With me here I have a bottle of Hennessy. I'm opening it up now for you, Tshif. I will pour half on your head. I'm pouring it now. Enjoy.

Okay, I'm leaving now. I'm supposed to be at your house for your After Tears. Your friend Matome must be wondering where I have got to. I left him under the big tree next to your house and told him that I was going to pick up a friend at the taxi rank. I had to come here alone to say my goodbyes.

Talk of the devil, here is Matome calling me again. Let me go and join him for your After Tears. We will drink the rest of this bottle of Hennessy under the tree while we play "Four Women" by Nina Simone. Yes, we will play "Four Women", your favourite tune.

THE GUMBOOT DANCER

It took about twenty knocks on my door, fifteen missed calls and five intercom calls to wake me up that Monday morning. At first it sounded like a dream. The intensity of the knocks progressed from mild to thunderous. Finally, I answered. They were about to leave me behind. I had spent the previous night drinking some lagers at Park Station's Buffalo Bills with my friend Vula. We only left at about three in the morning. Upon coming back to my Braamfontein apartment on De Korte Street, I had planned to sleep for two hours, wake up at five and have a shower. I thought I would be ready by the time they came to pick me up to go to the airport at six. I was wrong. I was fast asleep when the driver and my friend Nazo came knocking at my door. My cell phone alarm rang unanswered, but they could tell I was inside because the key was in the lock of my front door.

By half past six I was in the minibus taxi laid on for us by the Department of Arts and Culture to drive us to OR Tambo airport. Everyone was neatly dressed, including my colleagues in the gumboot dance club. My friend Kabelo was there too. He lived in the nearby suburb of Xavier. The other people in the other taxi were government officials and Members of Parliament that I didn't know. There were about eight of us, selected to represent South Africa in Mauritius. I was the leader of the gumboot dance club.

I was the last one to be picked up, and I still smelt of alcohol and smokes. I hadn't even had the chance to brush my teeth, let alone pack my clothes. There was no way I could have missed that Mauritius trip.

"We nearly left you behind, buddy," said Nazo as he gave us the itinerary.

"I'm sorry."

I looked at the itinerary and realised that we were scheduled for dinner with the Mauritian Minister of Arts and Culture that evening. All I had in my bag was a pair of shorts, a pair of jeans, three T-shirts and my gumboots. I had even forgotten to bring underwear, and the pair of dirty red Converse that I was wearing was my only pair of shoes. I also didn't have enough cash in my account. Luckily we were given a stipend in US dollars at the airport, but I didn't have time to go to the shops.

I was the most disorganised in that group, and had even forgotten to bring my yellow fever card, which was a requirement before I could be allowed to check in. When I went to the airport clinic, I hoped that my name would appear on the files, as I had used the same clinic on a recent trip to Tanzania. But the doctor informed me that the 2008 files were missing, and therefore they could not confirm my name or give me any discount. He also told me that the doctor who used to work there had disappeared with the files, as he was being investigated by the government for medical aid fraud. I ended up paying five hundred rands for a new card.

There was a long queue at the foreign exchange counter, as well as at the airport clinic, where I eventually got my yellow fever injection. By the time I boarded the plane, everyone was already seated. I must have been the last passenger, as I heard my name being called repeatedly on the speakers.

I slept most of the way, and even missed breakfast. When we landed in Mauritius, we went to La Maurice Hotel. At the dinner I was an embarrassment. I was dressed in jeans and a T-shirt with the words: *You can have this body if you want.* Everyone else was dressed up.

After the dinner with the minister, we went back to the hotel. Kabelo and I decided to stop by the bar. While we were having a drink, some ladies came by. We concentrated on two who walked with haughty steps. One was wearing a turquoise daisy blockprint shoulder dress with a front drape neckline and padded shoulders. She had a huge Afro on her oval face. The taller one had plaited hair and wore a red swirl-stripe dress with a sheared elastic self-tie neckline. They both carried beautiful three-tone handbags. The Afro girl's lime-green slingback shoes made more noise than the other one's taupe open-toe low heels. They knew we were whispering about them. Kabelo was still in his beautiful charcoal slim-fit suit, a white wing-collar dress shirt, black bow tie and black Pierre Cardin leather lace-up shoes. The two ladies smiled at the compliments he showered on them, but they seemed to be ignoring me. Then he decided to lure them to our table and indulged them with some strawberry daiquiris and piña coladas.

"May I have the honour of knowing you, beautiful ladies?" he purred, switching on the charm.

"My name is Kina and my friend is Grace."

"Where are you beautiful ladies from?" he asked the one with plaited hair after she had taken a few sips of her daiquiri.

"I'm from Uganda, and Grace is from Tanzania," she replied, turning to her oval-faced friend.

"I thought you both came from one country."

"No." She stressed the word with a flutter of her eyelashes. "Actually we met on the plane." She paused. "I flew via Dar."

Grace smiled, showing a golden tooth wedged between her other teeth. We sat with the two ladies drinking until about ten. We learnt that they, like us, were there on some cultural invitation. After ten o'clock we decided to go to Kina's room to continue drinking. It seemed like Kina was enjoying Kabelo a lot, as she blushed each time she spoke to him. Most girls in Jozi liked Kabelo. His voice was quiet and his manners were refined. He had a thin, clean-shaven face. On the other hand, Grace was obviously disappointed at being matched with me, and I could tell that she liked my friend as well.

The hotel had supplied two free bottles of wine in each room. Before we finished the wine, Grace left us to go to her room. I didn't even look at her as she walked away. Anyway, she was slender and small-breasted. Not my type. She also had a toothpick-wide gap between her front teeth. Kabelo decided to go fetch his two free bottles, as his room was closer than mine.

The thing about Kabelo is that he is not a drinker. He is also an obsessive anti-smoker, but he enjoys the company of beautiful ladies a lot. Actually he has a number of them in Joburg. That night he managed to drink two glasses of wine and coasted on those for several hours. He refilled Kina's glass as soon as it was empty. Then he went to fetch two more bottles.

"Don't be late," she said to him as he got up and moved towards the door.

"I won't," he replied, opening the door. "Please miss me when I'm gone. And don't do anything I wouldn't do."

"Never," she said, her eyes travelling over his body as he left the room.

Kina's eyes gazed at the door as it closed. Her lips curled in a slow smile. Then she bent forward, as if to suppress a belch, before turning to me.

"Do you think he likes me?" she asked, her face lighting with a slow smile.

I walked slowly to the window and opened it. I lit a cigarette. The grey coils of smoke rose slowly from my fingers and vanished in the pure air of her room.

"What do you mean?" I said with narrowed eyes.

She looked at me thoughtfully. Her eyes widened, and her smile wobbled. Then she looked at the almost empty bottle and topped up her already full glass. From the window I could hear the wine trickle musically into the glass.

"Well, he hasn't said anything yet to me, but I can see that he is a friendly guy," she said, a bit distractedly, glancing at the door and giving ear to the sound of footsteps outside.

"Well, I think he likes you. But he hasn't said anything because he is gay."

She looked at me fixedly. Then she slowly picked up her glass and took a long sip. I watched as she put the glass down and leaned back in her chair. Her arms were folded across her chest and her head slightly tilted. She gazed at me with a shocked expression.

"He is gay?" she repeated blankly.

"Very gay."

"Are you serious?" she asked, and her voice and manner demanded truthful answers.

"I'm definitely sure. I mean, he is my friend after all."

My reply silenced her for a few seconds. I looked at her and saw her forehead wrinkle with uncertainty. She cocked her head as though listening to distant music. Then she bit her lips and shut her eyes before shaking her head from side to side.

"Well, he's not yet open about it," I added. "But he is gay."

"What a waste!" she said, sounding disappointed.

"Why do you say that?" I asked, looking as though it were the most unreasonable statement in the world.

"Because he is such a hot brother, you know. Gayism and lesbianism means a freeway straight to hell," she said, raising her eyebrows.

"What? Where do you get that now?" I asked, clearly offended that "hot brother" was not directed at me.

"Don't you know?" she asked, and without waiting for my response added, "being gay or lesbian is a sin. Period."

"Judging other people is a sin as well, did you know that?" I said. "We must allow people to be real and honest about who they are. I don't believe that a person just wakes up one day and decides to be either gay or lesbian. I believe they are born that way. If God didn't want gays and lesbians he would not have allowed one to have feelings for the same sex."

Stunned, she was silent for a few seconds. The question that she seemed about to ask me had gone. Instead she opened her mouth briefly. As I extended my hand to pick up my glass, she examined my fingers closely.

"Are you gay?"

"No. Why?"

"Are you Christian?"

I parted my lips to answer, and then held back the words. She was still looking at me as though I would have committed the worst crime imaginable by admitting to being both gay and not Christian.

"No, I'm not Christian either."

"But do you believe in God?"

"No, but I'm afraid of Him."

"Then I'm not surprised. Gay people must pray hard to get rid of that disease." She paused. "Oh God Almighty, have mercy! This world is really coming to an end. Jesus is indeed coming back soon."

"That's a lie the Christians have been telling us for ages now. I mean, nobody told you to be straight and have feelings for the opposite sex. So you must stop judging and hating others because you have your own sins as well. Let homosexuals live their lives. Why do we judge? After all, we are all children of God."

"I suggest you read Leviticus 18:22, my South African brother. It will tell you that if a man has sexual relations with another man, they have a disgusting thing, and both shall be put to death for they are responsible for their own death."

"What? That's the same reason I'm not interested to read it."

She ignored me, took her glass and raised it to her nose. She inhaled deeply. Then she screwed her face up as the brutal words rushed forth.

"Let me enlighten you. The same reason why God destroyed

Sodom and Gomorrah was because of the gay lifestyle." She snapped her fingers and heaved her shoulders up and down. "Gays are agents of darkness, my brother. That is why we refer to rape as sodomy. It is taken from the act of Sodom. This is the same reason why God had to destroy Gomorrah and Sodom. The devil is playing with people's lives. Oh God, have mercy on us! You must read Revelation 22:11 as well. I can see that you like defending the wrong things. Maybe you're also gay. Why are most South African men gay?"

"Me? No, I'm not. I'm actually interested in you," I said with perceptible reluctance. "But I saw the way you looked at Kabelo and thought, well . . . Anyway, just so you know, he has come with his boyfriend here."

"Really?" she asked, pursing her lips.

"Yes. But please don't tell him anything. Like I said, he's still not open about his sexual orientation." I touched her hand. "And he is acutely sensitive."

"I won't say a word. Thanks for telling me this."

She looked at me sternly, her eyes narrowing but saying nothing. We heard footsteps in the passage, and looked up as Kabelo nudged the door open with his shoulder. Two wine bottles were in his right hand. He was talking on his phone. He put the bottles on the table and ended the call. He was courteous and charming with Kina as he removed the cap from one and poured her some wine. I could see that Kina had changed after our gossip. She was now studying his laugh and his mannerisms when he talked, as if these would reveal his gay status. The thing about Kabelo is that he has a soft, well-mannered voice, whereas mine is deep and throaty, almost rough. He is also an organised, businesslike type who hardly ever uses slang or swear words. But he is not gay.

"What is the gay community in South Africa like?" she asked out of the blue as soon as Kabelo sat down. "In Uganda we still have the issue of tolerance."

Kabelo looked at her, dumbfounded. I found the conversation very embarrassing. I threw her a wink, and then a scowl to keep quiet. She took the cue by picking up the glass. There was silence as we waited for her to take a slug of wine. But she put the glass down and looked at Kabelo intently. She was unsmiling, her eyes fixed on him in total attention. Strangely, I still found her excitingly desirable even after all she had said.

"South Africa is a democratic country," he corrected her with a hint of annoyance. "We recognise the rights of every individual. We are not as barbaric as Uganda, which persecutes gay and lesbian people."

I nodded my head gravely in agreement. She blinked in disbelief and knitted her brows. I wrinkled my brows too and made signs to her to drop the subject.

"It's amazing how most cute guys are gay, isn't it?" she said, feigning a smile. "Also how South Africa tolerates gay people."

"Why is that amazing for you?" he asked, his thin lips frozen in a half-smile.

"Because in Uganda we don't have such a thing," she said, and then paused. "I mean, gay people are lost in the matrix of self-identity. What they are doing is against the Bible. The problem with you South Africans is that white people have been fucking you up with apartheid for a long time. Now you are taking Western cultures into Africa."

Kabelo's mouth opened wide. He tilted his head back and rolled his eyes. Kina's sneer deepened under the influence of the mixed drinks working on her temper.

"My God! What is wrong with you?" he asked, half-offended. "Did someone shit on your dessert this evening? I can't believe you have just said that." He shook his head. "For your information, there is a study showing that in Uganda, where you say you come from, King Mwanga II of Buganda was known as the 'gay king'. He reportedly had sexual relations with men. I wonder if you know that little piece of your history."

"What?" she asked in surprise, her voice rising accusingly. "That is a colonial myth to —"

"And amongst the Nilotic-Langa in Uganda, men who appropriated a different gender status were known as 'mukododako'," he said, extending his right hand for emphasis. "These men were treated as women and permitted to marry other men."

Kabelo glanced searchingly at her and then at me. He shrugged, and then was silent. He stared at her without speaking. A tide of shame swept over me again. There was a long pause while we examined each other.

"That is a lie by the white man," she objected, frowning.

I looked at Kabelo, pleading with him not to speak further on the matter. Moving my eyes to Kina, I could see that her lips still shaped the last words that she had spoken as she waited for Kabelo's response.

"But there is evidence. You can't just say that this is a lie," he said with refined politeness. "The study also shows that in the Iteso communities in the northwest of Kenya and Uganda, same-sex relations existed amongst men who behaved as women and were socially accepted as women. Also in the Banyoro, the Langi in pre-colonial Benin, homosexuality was seen as a phase that boys had to pass through and grew amongst the Nandi and Kisii of Kenya, Igbo in Nigeria, Nuer of Sudan, and the Kuria of Tanzania."

His references to history made me think he was airing his superior education. Kina scowled at him. When she looked at me I pulled my eyes away and looked at the window. Then she raised her forehead thoughtfully.

"You don't believe that, do you?" she said with some appearance of scorn. When no one answered her, she continued. "I mean, I can't imagine some gay guy ramping up promotional propaganda aimed at abolishing our idea of family like I saw some disgusting South African gays marching in the street," she continued contemptuously. "Gays are calling for rights to foster their values and conditions on everyone else."

"No ... but you ... listen." I tried to speak. "No ... nonsense. You can never – "

She interrupted me before I could say what I wanted to say. Kabelo looked so upset that he could hardly find the words to express his rage. He briefly put his head in his hands.

"Why can't they simply just go on and remain in quiet solitude, or seclusion?" she continued with renewed determination. "So long as we keep sex private and not hear gay people walking down Broadway and calling on everyone to embrace their novel lifestyle."

"Who does that anyway?" I asked.

"I heard people claim that being gay is part of nature, and that God decides who a gay is. But for me, anything that comes at the back is rape. It is a white man's disease and you South Africans are afraid of the white man."

Kabelo frowned and clenched his jaw tightly.

"That is why you don't have your land back," she went on, "you are afraid of white people. There are just so many of them in your country and they enjoy it like they are in Europe. That is why it took you very long to have a black president like Mandela."

By this time Kabelo's nostrils were opening and shutting like gills. His expression became stern and serious. It was obvious that he had completely lost interest in her. I watched his shoulders sag as if under the weight of her ignorance. His face was tight with bewilderment and a growing anger that he was trying to suppress. He squeezed his hand on his forehead and tilted his head backwards.

"I can't believe you just said that," he said to her with a frown. "When I saw you earlier on I thought you were smarter than that. But like they say, you can't tell the height of a tree by the size of its shade. But you can't keep saying that homosexuality is a white man's disease. For your information, in the late 1640s a Dutch military attaché documented Nzinga, a warrior woman in the Ndongo Kingdom of Mbundu, who ruled as king rather than a queen." He nodded his head emphatically. "She used to dress as a man and surrounded herself with a harem of young men who dressed as women and who were later wives."

"He is right," I tried to intervene pacifically. "Look at Queen Modjadji in Bolobedu, for instance. She is married to women.

She is a lesbian. And there is a rumour that even Gandhi himself was gay."

He shook his head and she raised an eyebrow in disdain.

"God Almighty!"

"The evidence is that on Tolstoy Farm near Johannesburg, Gandhi forced his wife and all the other women to sleep without men in separate bedrooms. But he and Hermann Kallenbach, a German bodybuilder, shared a bedroom."

"How does that make him gay?"

"He wrote that sex between man and woman is the most revolting thing on earth. He even wrote to Kallenbach saying 'more love, yet more love, this is the love that the world has never seen. You have taken over my body totally. This is slavery with revenge'."

"No matter how much you guys can justify it, homosexuality is a mental illness." She paused while tapping her head with a finger to emphasise mental illness. "An ass is never a sexual organ. And very soon they will rape young children."

Kabelo clapped his hands together in a gesture of bafflement. He looked earnestly into her eyes. She picked up her glass of wine and swallowed the contents in one go. One bottle was finished, and her glass was empty. He didn't refill it for her.

"Homosexual adults are not attracted to children, my dear. Like you and I, they are attracted to adults," he said with great calmness. "And for your information, heterosexuals can also pose more of a threat to children. Also, if you think that homosexuality does not occur in nature, then you're wrong. There is scientific research that shows that homosexuality is found in many species besides human beings."

His words seemed to strike some deep chord in her. She listened to him with piercing attention. I exchanged quick glances with her, consciously devoid of meaning. She said nothing, but coughed once. I looked down.

"You see," she said, pointing at him, "I also couldn't believe when I heard that you were gay."

I cringed. Kabelo pulled a face as if something was hurting him. She grinned and winked at me. Kabelo's steady gaze never left her face. He glanced at me with a look of deep distrust. I felt a wave of guilt.

"What? Who told you that?" he asked. There was a peculiar tone of disbelief in his voice.

His eyes settled on me accusingly. I forged some furrows on my forehead and shook my head as Kina looked at me briefly. Kabelo looked hard at me.

"Nobody told me," she said hesitatingly, as if repressing an impulse to call him a pervert. "Let's just say that I know how gay people talk and walk."

I was expecting an outburst, but instead he just raised an eyebrow, shrugged and made no comment. He moistened the screen of his Samsung S4 phone with his own spit and slowly wiped its surface. Then his long restrained irritation suddenly burst out.

"I think you guys are too drunk to talk to," he said, and pointed a finger accusingly at me. "Vusi, you are a pathetic cock-block! And as for you, Kina," pointing at her, "your opinion is bigoted. Jesus said, 'Come as you are, and you'll be loved.' So, your reference to the Bible and nature is very wrong. You must get your facts right next time."

"Being black, white or any other colour is natural," she said, looking around and snapping her fingers. "Mixing colours or same sex is not natural. You gay people act as if what you're doing is natural."

Before Kabelo could answer, his phone rang. He picked it up and rose to his feet.

"Hello babe."

He talked on the phone while he walked towards the door. He chuckled softly as he spoke, with wrinkles forming at the corners of his eyes. Kina looked at him, smiled slightly awkwardly, and returned her eyes to her empty glass. I refilled it. Kabelo finished the call, and his mind seemed to be elsewhere. He opened the door to leave.

"Good night, guys," he said, and without waiting for our reply added, "You guys have a lot in common."

"See you at breakfast," I said, feeling uncomfortable under his stare.

Kina followed him with her eyes. When she turned to look at me, I smiled and adjusted my chair to sit next to her.

"Gays are perverts!" she said rudely and flatly as Kabelo stood in the doorway.

Pretending he had not heard her, he closed the door and walked away down the passage.

"You're very fascinating, you know that?" I said. "Very fascinating indeed."

It was supposed to be a compliment, but she brushed it aside with a wave of her hand. She looked at me hard as if reading my face. Suddenly I could hear her lips come close to my ear.

"Do you have a son, or a baby brother?" Her voice was serious and demanding.

"Yes, why?" My curious eyes rested on her face and on her plaited hair.

"Gays are paedophiles who will soon molest you or your son or baby brother," she said with the firmness of self-conviction. "You must be careful of people like him around your little brother."

I was dumbfounded. She bit her lip, realising she had perhaps said too much. She lifted her glass and sipped tentatively. Then she put the glass down.

"Why discriminate against people on the basis of their sexuality?" I asked, looking at her with a sudden manufactured irritation.

She twisted from side to side. Her wide-set eyes looked keenly and calmly into mine.

"Because their kind of relationship is not allowed even in the kingdom of animals." She paused as if contemplating her own words. "The Westerners are foolish people. Very soon they will legalise marriage to insects. Our African culture forbids it. We did not inherit it from our ancestors."

She said the last two sentences rapidly, without thinking. I was watching her closely. She raised her glass to her lips, but decided against drinking immediately.

"Tell me one more last thing," she said, pointing at the door as if Kabelo was still there. "Is he a he or is he a she to his babe, or is she a he or he a she? I'm just curious, you know."

Her mouth twisted into a mocking smile, and I was confused. She looked at me for a moment, half inquiringly, half as if she was angry that I was not answering her. Instinctively, I shot out one hand, grasped hers firmly and covered it with the other. That touch sent a keen pang of lust through me.

"Okay, will you do that research for me?" she said.

"You are one hell of a woman," I said, smiling at her.

"I'm just curious to know what he feels when he sees a beautiful woman like me," she said confidently.

Then she looked at me and smiled. I felt hypnotised. She leant forward, and watched me intently. The smile was still on her lips.

"Oh, really?" I said, suppressing a nasty laugh.

"That's all I want to know," she said, drawing a breath and nodding her head defiantly.

"But you don't have to look that far to feel that," I whispered, touching her affectionately on the arm. "I'm here."

She blushed and smiled understandingly. It was one of those rare smiles, with a quality of eternal reassurance in it.

"Oh, what do you do in South Africa?" she asked, genuinely interested.

"I work for the government."

"Doing what exactly?" she asked suspiciously.

I didn't want to tell her that I was a gumboot dancer in case it didn't sound attractive. I looked at her closely for a while. There was a single jet-black strand of hair out of place.

"I'm working as an advisor in the Ministry of Arts and Culture," I said, a little shocked at how easily the lie slipped out.

"That is interesting," she said thoughtfully. "But there is a lot of crime in South Africa. Not so very long ago we saw some people burning a foreigner. South Africans are very xenophobic."

"Well, it was an unfortunate incident. Every country has its own bad people, and I'm totally ashamed of it as well."

"But you South Africans are conceited. You forget how other countries have helped you when the whites were oppressing you. Now that you have your freedom you forget a lot. You have dementia."

I cleared my throat and tried to change the topic. Then I stood up and went to the window. Looking out at the darkened ocean, I lit a cigarette. I puffed while arranging an opinion in my mind. She came over, lit a cigarette and stood next to me. I puffed again, looking at her with admiration.

"Are you married?" I asked after a brief pause.

"No."

"Are you in a relationship?"

"I was. But we have just separated."

"Do you have kids?"

"Yes. I have a beautiful daughter," she said, smiling radiantly at me. "She is seven years old. I also have another daughter I have adopted."

"You seem to like kids. At least we have something in common."

"I seem to like kids?" she laughed delightedly, which only increased my lust for her. "I love kids. Well, I have adopted my late sister's daughter." She paused. "And you, do you have kids and a wife?"

"I have a son, yes, but no wife. I think I must negotiate with you to be his future mother, and we can make more kids together."

The blush that had risen to her face a few moments before turned into a bewitching smile. On an impulse I reached out and ran my finger over her lips.

"Nice try, but sorry."

"Why not?"

"Because a long-distance relationship is not my idea."

"I'm prepared to leave my job and come to Uganda."

"How are you going to look after me if you quit your job, silly man?" She shook her head.

"I will write articles for international newspapers, like I'm already doing."

Her face brightened. My eyes were directed at her cleavage.

"You have answers for everything, don't you?"

"I'll kiss my future wife for that true observation."

She was astounded, and I could see that her admiration for me had doubled. I kissed her well-powdered face. She responded. The warmth, fragrance and colour of her body appealed to my senses. The next thirty minutes were spent with my right hand on her left thigh, alternately massaging the nape of her neck. The fires of my lust began to glow angrily in my veins. I poured her another glass of wine. We subsided into silence and sweet anticipatory thoughts. I tilted the glass towards her mouth. After she had taken a sip, I leant forward and kissed her, slowly.

"Wait," she said. "This is not right. I mean, we just met today and now we are doing this."

"Don't worry, baby," I said, with the fires of lust springing up in me again. "This is the best way of knowing each other."

She gazed at me with a moody, puzzled expression. It was the kind of signal that women looking for casual sex send out to show that they are open to it. I kissed her hard on the mouth, and she responded. I tenderly clasped her by the neck, and she laid her face upon my chest. What she whispered in my ear seconds later was as sweet as the sound of the word "heaven" in a believer's ear.

THE BABY SHOWER

For eight months now I have tried to forget everything about you. Until last week. When I bumped into someone that you used to know. It was your old friend Fefe. She mentioned your name, of course. Your name which is no longer part of my vocabulary.

I met Fefe at uShaka Marine World in Durban. She said she had come down for the Easter holiday with her friends. You know how Joburgers are – they always come to the coast to drink beer and make noise with their loud car speakers. Fefe and I talked for about thirty minutes, and it was all about you. Surprisingly, this time I didn't react to your name in the way I have become accustomed to. Six months ago, at some restaurant in the Gateway Mall, I was served by a waiter with your name pinned to her chest. You won't believe what I did. Yes, I stormed out of the restaurant without eating the food that I had ordered. And, more recently, at a Total filling station in Pietermaritzburg, I left without petrol for the same reason. Your name was mentioned by one of the petrol attendants as he came to help me and it felt like both my eardrums were about to burst.

This weekend, after talking with Fefe, I was so overwhelmed by thoughts of you that I drove from Durban to Jozi. As I drove slowly along the street in Katlehong where we used to live, memories and images of you replaced one another with extraordinary swiftness in my mind. Nothing but sad memories.

There are new people living in our house now. They have built a carport next to what used to be our bedroom, but otherwise everything looks just the same.

So you might be wondering why I haven't called you. The truth is that I still have not forgiven you. How can I? When you called me on 10 June, a year and a half ago, with the good news, I was the happiest man alive. You were released from the hospital in Ermelo, you said. It was a boy, you told me. He had come a bit earlier than we had expected. You had previously told me that you were due around 15 July.

You were on your way back to your mother's place as per our agreement when I spoke to you. We had wanted you to get all the motherly support you could during the last weeks of your pregnancy and in the days after the birth. That was why you left Katlehong a month before our son was born.

Our home was very quiet after you left and I was looking forward to your return. I even suggested that we get a helper for you, but you refused vehemently. You said it would be very expensive and convinced me that you would prefer to stay with your mother in Wesselton. I understood. Your mother is a nurse at the hospital in Ermelo, so it made sense that you would want to stay with her.

We communicated regularly as the pregnancy advanced. I couldn't wait for 15 July, the date the doctors had given you as the birth date of our son.

Then I got a call from you on 9 June. You sounded weak. You told me that your water had broken. I wanted to come to Ermelo immediately and be with you. I wanted to witness the arrival of my precious angel, to share the pain and the joy with you, but you were very much opposed to my idea. Among other things, you were afraid that the township boys would steal our things while I was away from the house. You convinced me that they would steal all the toys and clothes that we had already bought for our son. You were right, I thought. The township boys had already stolen our flatscreen TV and the Apple laptop that I had bought you. They had even stolen your underwear from the washing line in the past. But I was still eager to come to Ermelo. So eager that I suggested that we get that quiet boy ... What was his name ...? Sello. Yes, Sello. That boy who stayed on the corner of our street to look after our house. You said no. You said that he would sleep with girls in our bedroom.

Although I doubted that Sello would do such a thing, you were right – one cannot trust township boys.

You promised to come home in a few days.

I waited impatiently for news that night. I couldn't sleep. Eventually I tried to call your cousin Mandisa, but her cell phone was off. I thought that something bad had happened to you and I was panicking. I'd heard stories about women dying after giving birth.

I finally received a call from Mandisa. It was about three in the morning when she told me that our baby had been born. I asked her for the details as I wanted to record the correct date and time in my diary. She simply responded that you had given birth an hour earlier. You don't know the joy that I felt when I recorded *two am, Ermelo Hospital, my boy, my king is born* in my diary. I even called my mother and woke her up with the joyous news. She immediately gave me our son's name: Xolani. Be at peace. The ancestors had answered our prayers, she said. She knew how hard we had tried to have a baby and all about your miscarriages.

Oh, the things we did to try and guarantee a healthy pregnancy! You were there when my mother and Uncle Skhu took me to meet my biological father in Isipingo, south of Durban. I had to change my surname from Manyisa to Sibeko. Uncle Skhu had insisted that nothing would be right unless I used my real father's last name. I had not met the guy before because my mother hated him for abandoning us. Once I had met him in Isipingo I had to undergo some stressful rituals. As a Christian, it was not easy for me to wear the isiphandla until it dried on my wrist. Imagine having to change my name at the bank, get a new ID, driver's license, certificates, a new signature at the age of thirty-one. But I wanted to appease my ancestors and when I reported to my mother and my uncle that you were pregnant a few months later, they insisted that I give thanks by slaughtering. The birth of Xolani was important to all of us.

I was anxious to see my baby and called you almost every hour that week. You still sounded very weak. I asked you to send me photos of him via MMS on your phone, but you said that flashing a camera at a newborn baby might not be a good idea. You also said that you could not travel in a taxi with a newborn. I really understood. I agreed to give you some money to hire a car to bring you home at the end of the month. That was another two weeks without seeing my son.

Like I told you, at work my colleagues were very happy for me. They could see how excited I was about Xolani's birth. I talked to my boss, Kecia, almost every day about him. She gave me advice on how I could plan for our son's future while he was still young. She even gave me toys that her five-year-old son, Brandon, had played with when he was a toddler. I also took out a subscription to a local parenting magazine because of her.

The day after you told me he had been born, I opened an account in his name at First National Bank for his future studies. I even bought some books on how to be a good parent.

The month of July lapsed and you still weren't home. I was losing patience with the situation. I wanted to see my son. You told me that Xolani was sick and had to go to the doctor. I put some money in your bank account. I was panicking, thinking that my baby would die before I saw him. I begged you to let me come over and see you both one weekend. I mean, Ermelo is not far, about three to four hours from Jozi. You explained that the sleeping arrangements were difficult at your mother's place. I told you that I would book a hotel, but you said no. You reasoned that our baby was crying a lot because he was so sick and they might not allow us to stay in the hotel, because of the noise he was making. After you heard me plead earnestly, you reluctantly agreed to arrange a place for me that coming weekend. We talked on Tuesday. On Friday I was preparing to catch an Ermelo taxi at Park Station when you called to say that your sister had arrived unannounced with her husband. You also made me speak to her, and she was very sorry. You promised that you'd come home the following day instead.

On Saturday, you told me that you were taking Xolani to the doctor again. He had developed thrush, you said. The good thing is that this time you sent me pictures of him from your cell phone. I was very happy to see my baby for the first time and immediately used one of the pictures as my screensaver. He looked very handsome with that little nose and broad forehead.

You and Xolani finally came home on 15 August, a windy Monday. He was exactly two months and five days old. I came home to find you there with him. He was sleeping in our bed. I hugged and kissed you; you were happy to be home. In the bedroom, you opened the blue blanket that covered his little face. My heart leapt with joy as I touched him for the very first time. I examined him adoringly. There was something striking in his appearance. He was big for a two-month-old baby. You were smiling. Those eyes are mine, big and round, I thought. You pointed at his little fat fingers and nails. They were daddy's fingers too. But the mouth was just like my mother's, wide and dark.

My friends came with gifts as soon as they heard that Xolani was home. Even my boss, Kecia, braved the township to bring us the gifts. You were pleasantly surprised that a white woman had come to the township to see our boy.

Then one night, a week after you had come home, Xolani started to cry when you were fast asleep. He cried nonstop. I didn't want to wake you up as you were sleeping peacefully, so I jumped up from our bed and walked to his cot. I turned him over, so that he could sleep face down, but he continued crying. I switched on the light, picked him up and began to rock him in my arms. He was quiet for about five minutes. I saw you lazily open your eyes. You mumbled something and then went back to sleep again.

I sat at the window, watching the morning invade our neighbourhood with Xolani still in my arms. He started crying again. I walked hastily up and down, hoping that you would wake up, but your mouth was wide open and you were snoring loudly. I thought that this must be what first-time mothers did, fresh from the pains of giving birth.

I took Xolani's bottle from the dressing table and gave it to him. The doctors had advised you that you didn't have enough milk, so we had decided to feed Xolani with a bottle. I was enjoying the joys of parenthood, watching my son feed, when he started choking and then vomiting. I must admit that I was alarmed. I woke you up.

As soon as you saw the quivering face of our son, you took him from me. We were both panicking. I thought we were losing him.

You stood there, patting him gently on the back until he stopped choking. But as you removed the last of the vomit from his mouth with your fingers, Xolani began to scream as if he was trying to tell us something. His little voice was becoming hoarse. You finally put your breast in his mouth, although you complained that there was only little milk. He kept quiet for a while as he suckled on your breast. We were relieved.

Less than ten minutes later Xolani started to scream again. You began to walk up and down the room with him, murmuring, "My big boy, Xoli. My big boy." That's what you said. I told you that I was going to call my mother and ask her about the ntlokwana ritual, which is traditionally performed by healers when a baby is young to make them strong. You were vehemently against it and even questioned whether I was a committed Christian. We then agreed to take the boy to the doctor instead. I wanted to go there with you, but you told me not to worry. No, I must go to work, you insisted.

Xolani began to sob piteously. You used my surname to make him stop, but he didn't. I was very scared. So were you. You brought out your breast and thrust it into his crying mouth once again. He choked a little bit, then stopped and burst out crying again.

I called you from work at about nine that morning, but your phone was off. I thought maybe our child had been admitted to hospital. I got very worried. Something was wrong, I could feel it. You phoned me about three hours later. You were crying hysterically as you told me the news. Our baby had been stolen. You were at Thokoza Police Station.

I immediately asked a colleague to drive me to Thokoza. Your version was that you gave Xolani to a woman who was posing as a nurse. She was wearing white, you said. You even described her to the police.

I called your mother to tell her what had happened, and she immediately drove down to Jozi. That night we went all over the place, asking people if they knew anything about what had happened. Your mother even called your ex-boyfriend Mxo, thinking that maybe he'd had something to do with it as he was very jealous, according to her. What worried me most was that Mxo admitted to having seen you when you were in Ermelo. I began to wonder if you had been with him all the time that you had been away from me, if you and Mxo were doing something behind my back. It bothered me like a pebble in a shoe.

We both prayed every day for our son to be returned. We even went to the sangomas. They all promised that Xolani was safe, but none of them could locate his whereabouts.

A month later, I discovered the truth. It shocked me. In fact, I don't think I will ever recover from it. That was the day I saw you in the magistrate's court. My heart bled as the journalists' cameras flashed. I stared at your face for a long time. Your eyes gave away no sign of emotion although the court gallery behind you was filled with relatives and friends. I could see your soul in the corner of your eyes, and I didn't like it. You looked away when the prosecutor began to outline the facts in your case. I pressed my palms to my ears as you held your head high, barely moving. I wanted to keep the sound out. I didn't want to hear any more of it. That is why I left. I didn't want to hear you confess, with an air of indifference, as they reported in the papers. Even now I'm still trying to banish the memory of that unpleasant day from my mind.

There are tales that get harder to understand the more they are told. I discovered this after you were committed to a psychiatric institution. I had many puzzles to solve. Only now does everything make sense to me.

I should have known that it was a lie when you told me that you were pregnant. My love for you made me naïve. The truth was right under my nose, but I was paying attention to the wrong clues.

I went to the hospital when you were so-called pregnant. The nurses told me that you were not on any of their lists. You came back later and I asked you where you'd been. You insisted that you had been at the hospital, but in the gynaecologist's consulting room. I believed you. You showed me the scans of our baby sitting comfortably in your tummy. I guess I was blinded by love. Love of you, love of our child.

I should have questioned you more intently when your stomach did not swell like it does with other pregnant women. You told me a story about your mother and said you had inherited your physique from her. She was still in school when she had you and she'd told you that no one had suspected her pregnancy until she gave birth.

I failed to read the signs when Xolani clamped his mouth around your dry nipple. I saw him turn his face away from your breast, but I was not brave enough to question you.

Every night I dream of a child crawling across the floor of my room on his hands and knees. Sometimes I dream about holding him close to my chest or of swinging him around, his little dimples deepening with every new smile.

How do you think people look at me now: my neighbours, my friends, my colleagues? Kecia, my boss, suggested that I go and see a psychologist. She gave me her psychologist's card. He had helped her when she'd lost her husband. I don't think you know this, but Kecia lost her husband and son Brandon in a horrible car accident about four months ago. It was all over the news. They were hit by a lorry that failed to stop at an intersection in Kempton Park.

The name of the psychologist that Kecia recommended is Dr Sweeney. She says he is very good, but how does she think I'm going to talk to a white man? My English is bad. How is he going to understand me when there are such barriers between us? Language. Culture. That is why I threw his card away. Of course, I didn't tell Kecia that I had thrown Dr Sweeney's card away. I just told her that I'm still saving money for the sessions. You know how white people are; they prefer talking to people in order to heal. I'm a black person and everything has to be linked to my ancestors. They are the ones with all the answers. I don't want a white doctor who will tell me the obvious.

The details from the courtroom are still fresh in my mind. Yes, you did go to the hospital that day and you did hand Xolani over to a woman. But that woman was not dressed in white. In fact, she was your cousin Mandisa. The CCTV footage shows her standing with her boyfriend, waiting for you. And Mandisa was not a stranger to Xolani. She was, in fact, our son's biological mother. She even breastfed Xolani in your presence. Like she said during the court proceedings, the two of you had agreed to meet every Wednesday in Bethal so that she could breastfeed Xolani. That is why you always came home very late on Wednesdays. But this time Xolani was sick, and you were afraid he was going to die. When Mandisa met you at Thokoza Hospital, the two of you had a disagreement and she threatened to take her baby back.

The CCTV footage shows her entering the hospital. Meanwhile, you were caught on camera making sure that people saw you with Xolani. You even took a picture of yourself with him at the hospital and put it up on your Facebook page.

I saw you sneering at Mandisa when she gave evidence in court. Mandisa said that she had given you the baby because she needed the money that you promised her. She kept referring to Xolani as Lwandle because that is his real name.

It was then that I came to the realisation that just about anything is possible if people are poor.

I could not believe it when you insisted to the court that Xolani was your baby. I was so surprised that I involuntarily glanced at your face. I must say that you did a good job of looking innocent. But those SMSes between you and your cousin spelled out the truth. How could you be so stupid? How did you feel as you stood in front of the magistrate and the text messages were read to you? I saw you looking around, your lips trembling as the text messages were read out:

> *You said you'll pay me one thousand every month. You haven't paid me this month. I want my baby back.*
>
> *Where is my baby? Is he growing? I must come to see him.*
>
> *I miss my Lwandle.*

I must confess that at that moment, I saw you as a snake baring its fatal fangs.

After you were locked away I still maintained contact with Mandisa and her parents. I hoped that somehow things might work out as I was still attached to Xolani. I bought clothes for him and every other weekend I would go and visit him in Ermelo. Mandisa's mother is still unemployed. Her father is also not working. He is isibotho. I even began to negotiate to adopt my boy, but Xolani's real father, Duma, is very angry. How can I be the father to his child? he asks.

I must admit that you have shaken my confidence in some important sense. You have made me believe that women can't be trusted.

I used not to sleep at night; I hardly ate anything and I prayed constantly. Uncle Skhu advised that I go and see a traditional healer and get a new girlfriend. My mother called you a witch. They all made sense to me. The ancestors were trying to communicate to me through what happened between us. Remember what I told you when we were trying hard to have a child? I told you that things were going wrong because I was not using my right surname. That is the reason I changed my name from Mohau Manyisa to Sabelo Sibeko.

Just so that you know, I'm here in KwaZulu-Natal now, Isipingo, where nobody will ever find me. I'm far away from you. You are part of an experience I'm still trying to blot out of my consciousness. My experience with you has taught me that there is no such thing as forgiveness. People just have short memories. You and I are history now. And, as they say, history is like a pot left on a stove by an absentminded chef with too much on her plate. Between you and me, I don't know which one of us is the chef.

AFFLUENZA

It was mid-afternoon when Fana entered the Sandton Square restaurant. Only a few customers were inside, scattered at the tables. A man was reading the *Mail & Guardian* at the far end of the restaurant, his glasses low across the bridge of his nose as he stared at the page intently. Three ladies with lovely complexions were sitting at the bar, laughing loudly and gesturing this way and that. As he entered, Fana became aware of the ladies, but he did not glance at them despite the murmur of admiration that erupted as soon as they spotted him. He had come straight from work and was still wearing his black pinstripe suit, teal shirt and maroon tie.

Fana took a seat in the corner of the restaurant so he could keep an eye on everyone coming in and out. He was waiting for his friend Sanele, who in just five short days was going to tie the knot with his sweetheart, Gontse, at the Regina Mundi Church in Soweto. Fana was Sanele's best man and had arranged a bachelor party for him in Mondeor that night. In fact, a few of their mutual friends were busy at that very moment hiring several ladies from Hillbrow's famous Royal Hotel to help them celebrate the end of Sanele's bachelorhood in style. Sanele was not aware of this, though. As far as he was concerned, he was meeting Fana for an evening out on the town.

While he waited, Fana decided to take a look at the present he had bought for his friend – a sketch of Sanele and his wife-to-be. It had been drawn by a Nigerian artist called Usoro. Fana had paid three hundred and fifty rand for it.

Fana took the sketch out of the tube that Usoro had given him to keep the artwork in pristine condition. Unrolling the sketch, he looked at it happily. It was the perfect gift for Sanele.

Slowly Fana allowed his eyes to wander in the direction of the ladies at the bar. One of them, wearing an elegant red dress, caught his stare and held it for a while before turning back to her friends. Fana pretended to go back to admiring the sketch that was still lying on the table in front of him, but in reality he was completely focused on eavesdropping on the ladies. They were talking about the value of an estate in Waterfall.

"It's worth more than ten million, I swear, my friendship," said the lady in the red dress. "Have you ever been inside? It's like being in a shopping mall."

"Not as big as Thabo's in Blue Downs," said the one sitting next to her. She was wearing a floral jumpsuit and her jet-black hair fell straight down her back. "Oh, my goodness!" She paused and took a deep breath. "Have you seen the car he drives? Aston Martin. He invited both Chris Brown and Rihanna to his birthday party and they sang privately for him. I was there. The dude is loaded, my friendship." She rubbed her thumb and forefinger together to indicate big money.

The ladies exchanged nods as Fana, pretending to be satisfied with his gift for Sanele, rolled the sketch back up and tucked it into the cardboard tube. As he finished putting the sketch away, he surreptitiously eyed the women at the bar. The lady in the floral jumpsuit was sipping a brown drink in a tall glass through a straw; her friend in the red dress was playing with a cherry that she had pinned between her long nails.

At that moment a young waitress with plump, dimpled cheeks approached Fana's table. "May I get you something to drink, sir?" she asked, raising her eyebrows at him. She had a Zimbabwean accent.

"Give me two fingers of Glenmorangie, please," he said in a loud voice, hoping the three ladies would hear him. "Put the ice in a separate glass."

As the waitress left his table, the lady in the floral jumpsuit turned her head briefly and looked in Fana's direction. Her face appeared baby soft, without a single blemish. A two-tone leather handbag was hooked over the back of her chair. As their eyes met, she pretended to be removing a strand of hair from her face, then she looked back at her friends. The topic of the conversation had changed to men, as if inspired by Fana's presence. He listened.

"Size makes no difference, my friendship," said the lady sitting opposite the one in the red dress. She was wearing a mint-coloured bead necklace over her turquoise midi dress. She had a face like a mannequin, her skin was very light in complexion and she had a high-pitched voice. "What's important are foreplay and passion," she continued, her hands moving as if she was conducting a choir. "Like they say, it's not the size of the ocean, but the motion of the ocean that counts."

There was laughter.

The waitress came with Fana's drink and put it in front of him. He gave a sigh of satisfaction as he raised the glass and inhaled the smell of the whisky.

"I disagree, my friendship," said the one in the floral jumpsuit. "I'm telling you that size is critical to pleasure. How can you reach orgasm if his thing is so small that he cannot reach your g-spot?" She spread her thumb and forefinger as if to indicate the minimum size required to bring her to climax. "It's impossible."

Red Dress laughed loudly while Mannequin Face swayed her head to and fro.

"I agree with Intle," Red Dress said. "Size is important. I had this boyfriend once who always bought me expensive clothes from overseas. I learnt to wear Gucci, Hugo Boss, Versace and Burberry through him." She pronounced the names of the brands as if she had never heard them said out loud before. "All those expensive labels. But the poor guy couldn't satisfy me in bed. Seriously, guys. I mean, he was useless."

"So you left him just because of that?"

"Of course."

"How do you leave such a providing man?" asked Mannequin Face. "He took great care of you, my friendship."

Before Red Dress could answer, Jumpsuit set her glass down and smacked her lips decisively. "Ah, my friendship. I'm tired of married men." She glanced at Fana. "I must get myself a Ben 10 who will be mine, and mine only."

The other two broke into peals of laughter and raised their glasses. Fana watched them furtively from the corner of his eye as he sipped his whisky.

"I used to have a Ben 10," said Mannequin Face, "but he was too much in love with his phone. He was nineteen when we met. I was twenty-nine. I bought him an iPhone, and I regretted it every day until we separated. That boy was always playing games and music on his phone, even when we were together. One day he even put his headphones on while we were making love. Never again will I date a baby."

The other two howled with laughter, banging the table and fighting for breath.

"Still, he used to give great massages," Mannequin Face continued when the laughter had died down, churning her drink around with the straw. "Sometimes non-sexual touching is more of a turn on."

"Guys are nowhere to be found nowadays," said Jumpsuit. "Either they are gay or happily married. One of the two. That is why I am looking beyond our borders. I started with a Zimbabwean, but it didn't work out. The one I have now is Nigerian, and though he has a habit of disappearing for a long time, at least, when he reappears, he always has lots of money to spoil me."

The lady in the red dress raised her head and her eyes met Fana's again for an instant, then she looked back down at her glass.

Swallowing the last of his drink, Fana motioned to the waitress. When she approached, he ordered another two fingers of Glenmorangie. As he did this he caught sight of the waitress's name-tag for the first time. Her name was Valentine.

"Were you born on the fourteenth of February?" Fana asked jokingly.

The waitress blushed. "No," she answered, shaking her head.

"Were you conceived on the fourteenth of that month?"

For a moment the waitress looked at him as if she didn't understand his question.

"No, it's just a name, sir," she finally said. "I was born on the twenty-ninth of July."

After the waitress had taken his order, Fana stood up and walked towards the smoking room. While sitting on the sofa he found inside, puffing his cigarette, he scrolled through his cell phone and ruminated a little. He read a new text message that had just come in from one of his friends, Santo. He had sealed the deal with the girls at the Royal Hotel and would be collecting five of them at six o'clock for the bachelor's party. Everything would be ready for Sanele's surprise by half seven.

Fana checked the time on his cell phone. It was sixteen minutes to four. Sanele would arrive at any moment.

As the waitress appeared with his drink and placed it on the table in front of him, the lady wearing the red dress walked into the smoking room, her stilettos making a clicking sound on the tiled floor. Looking up, Fana realised for the first time just how short her dress was. The extra attention probably makes her feel good, he thought. Between her fingers she was holding a long Vogue cigarette. She coughed delicately before asking Fana for a light.

"Great day, isn't it?" she said as Fana took out his gold lighter.

"Yes, it is," he replied.

Red Dress inhaled deeply and then exhaled with satisfaction.

"What are you beautiful ladies doing here on your own?" Fana asked.

"Ag, we're just chilling. I haven't seen my buddies in a long while," she said, blinking through the haze of smoke coming from her cigarette. "By the way, my name is Aya."

The corner of her mouth crinkled a little as she shook Fana's hand. Her eyes were large. Her nails were perfect.

"I'm Fana."

"Coming from work?" she asked, leaning against the window that framed the giant Mandela statue that dominated the square.

"Yes. I work here, at Alexander Forbes."

"I see," she said placidly. "Are you waiting for someone?"

"A friend of mine."

Aya finished her cigarette and stubbed out the butt in the silver ashtray next to Fana. He eyed her behind approvingly as he watched her leave the room. The way she swayed her hips exaggeratedly from side to side reminded him of how he had met Tulamo three years earlier at the Busy Corner Shisanyama in Ebony Park, near Tembisa. She was dancing to "Ingoma" by Thandiswa Mazwai, her buttocks moving rhythmically to the song as she sang along. They had been together ever since.

Five minutes later Fana was also done smoking. As soon as he shut the glass door of the smoking room behind him, he could hear that the ladies were talking about marriage. Sitting down at his table, he continued scrolling through his cell phone, taking the occasional sip from his glass.

"I guess sometimes you have to kiss a frog to find your prince," Mannequin Face said. "Maybe one day you will find Mr Right."

"I'm not looking for Mr Right," Aya said, shaking her head. "I've learnt the value of compromise. I'm getting older now and I want to settle down. All I want is a mature guy."

"Yes! When life gives you lemonade, you must add some vodka

and ice, my friendship," Jumpsuit said. "So when life gives you Mr Wrong, with potential, you can fine tune him into Mr Right."

The ladies laughed expansively and then, almost simultaneously, took a sip from their respective glasses. As they did this Valentine, the waitress, approached Fana's table.

"The lady over there says you are welcome to join them," she said to him in a low voice.

"Oh," Fana said, rubbing his chin. "Are you sure?"

Before the waitress could reply, Fana's eyes again met Aya's. A well-timed nod and a flutter of her eyelashes convinced him that what the waitress had told him was true.

"Give me another round, please," he said to Valentine as he stood up and began to walk towards the ladies. "And another one each of whatever the ladies are having."

As soon as he had joined the ladies, the sweet smell of their perfumes saluted Fana's nose.

"Thanks for agreeing to join us. This is my friend Intle," said Aya, gesturing to the lady in the floral jumpsuit. "And this is Sami." She pointed at Mannequin Face.

Fana smiled as he reached out to shake hands with both of the ladies. "Thanks for inviting me."

"No worries. We were just talking about you," Aya said. "I work in fashion. I was saying that you've got a body that I can sell."

"You think so?"

"Absolutely," Intle said quickly.

"May I have a look at that, please?" asked Sami, pointing at the tube that held Sanele's sketch.

"I own a modelling agency in Rosebank," Aya said, stretching her fingers out towards her glass as Fana passed Usoro's work over to Sami. "That is why I can confidently tell you what will work and what won't. Your body is perfect. Here is my business card." She handed Fana her card. "Imagine him paired with Nkele in that campaign we are doing!"

"Mmmm! That would be amazing!" Intle said, dropping her soft voice an octave.

The waitress came with their drinks as Sami unrolled the sketch. The air between them was immediately saturated with the aroma of expensive alcohol. Fana read Aya's business card: *Aya Kunene. CEO. Buhle Consultants. Rosebank.*

"Is this you?" asked Sami, referring to the sketch.

"No. It's a gift for my friend. He is getting married next week."

"Wow! So beautiful!"

"I hope he likes it," Fana said, an expression of pleasure flickering across his face. "He will be joining me here soon."

"It's amazing."

"Thanks. Are you also in the modelling business?"

"Me, no." Sami shook her head. "I'm a fashion designer."

"I see. How about you?" Fana asked Intle, giving his glass a twirl that made the ice cubes tinkle.

"I'm also a fashion designer."

At that moment Fana's phone rang. He excused himself, standing up to answer the call.

"I'm inside," he said, stroking his chin. "I can see you at the door. Look for the corner where the ladies are sitting."

Still standing, Fana drained his glass as he dropped the call. Turning back to the ladies, he saw that they were all focused on the entrance to the restaurant. A figure was just visible through the half-opened door. He was wearing a tan windbreaker and a lime shirt.

"Is that the guy you were talking to on the phone?" asked Intle as Sanele entered the restaurant and started towards their table with his rapid, rolling, bouncy step.

"That's him."

More drinks were ordered as soon as the ladies had finished greeting Sanele. Fana's friend preferred red wine.

"Maybe you ladies can help us later?" Fana said as soon as Valentine disappeared to fetch their order. "We are supposed to be finalising the programme for his wedding." Fana pointed at Sanele. "We think we've covered everything, but I am sure there are gaps. Maybe you can help us identify them?"

"Congratulations," said Intle with something akin to admiration in her eyes.

"Thanks," said Sanele, pressing his hands to his chest in gratitude. "But that can wait for now. Let me catch up with you guys by drinking first."

As he said this, Valentine appeared with a wine bottle and a glass. Setting the glass down in front of Sanele, she uncorked the bottle and poured a small amount for him to taste. Fana looked at his watch – it was almost twenty past four.

"I tell you what, guys. Why don't you ladies join us tonight for some more drinks?" Fana said as Sanele drank from his glass and nodded to the waitress. "We have a party going on later. I'm really enjoying your company."

"Really?" asked Aya in a high voice as Valentine filled Sanele's glass.

"Yes, it would be an honour," Fana said, searching each of the ladies' eyes for agreement.

"Well, I don't know about you," said Aya, glancing at Intle and then at Sami, "but that's cool with me. As long as we can stop off at my place first. I want to change into something more comfortable."

"And what about you two? Are you joining us?" Fana asked.

Intle nodded her confirmation, but Sami seemed hesitant. "Well, I don't know," she said doubtfully. "I have an important meeting tomorrow morning and I need to be fresh for it. Maybe I will just come for a couple of hours, but I also need to go home and change first."

"Okay, that's decided, then," Fana said. "Let's finish our drinks and get on the road. We need to be at the party by half seven. Where is your place?"

"Bez Valley."

"Well, that's on our way. The party is in Mondeor."

They left the restaurant fifteen minutes later – it was just after five o'clock in the afternoon. Outside, lightning flashed threateningly across the sky. It was clear that a big storm was brewing.

"It was nice meeting you guys," Sami said as she slung her handbag over her shoulder. "I will see you at the party."

"Likewise," said Sanele.

About thirty minutes later they arrived outside an old house in Bez Valley. Aya had led the way in her Audi Q5, Intle had joined Sanele in his Merc and Fana had driven alone in his Golf 6. As Fana stepped out of his car his phone rang again – it was Santo.

"Where are you, man? I've got the ladies and we are on our way to the venue!"

"In thirty minutes we'll be there," said Fana as he closed the door to his car. "Keep our guests entertained in the meantime."

"Please come inside," said Intle anxiously. "It's not safe to stand around on the street here. We won't take long, I promise."

The two men followed the ladies through the gate, Fana still on his cell phone. The house was run down and overshadowed by a ruined block of flats with peeling paint and leaking pipes.

"Shall we bring our swimming costumes as well?" Aya asked as she closed the gate behind them. "I love swimming when having drinks."

"Great idea! There is a swimming pool at the place we are going," said Fana, still on his cell phone.

Aya unlocked the door. "Come in, please," she said, ushering them inside.

There was a heavy smell of marijuana in the kitchen, which struck Fana as strange, but the whisky in his bloodstream and the possibility of wild lovemaking overtook any sense of foreboding that he might have had. He reached out to pass a hand over Sanele's head, a pacifying gesture. Sanele followed, hesitantly.

As soon as they were all inside Intle and Aya went to the bedroom. Fana and Sanele sat down on the black leather sofa in the sitting room. The walls were plastered, but free of pictures. A clock hung next to the old oak wall unit in which sat a battered-looking Sanyo hi-fi. Fana's eyes wandered from one corner to another. Joburg people! he thought. Why would a person buy such an expensive car but live in a place like this? He shook his head.

This is Johussleburg and everyone here is suffering from affluenza. Almost every black person pretends to be rich while staying in a rented room. Didn't he just pay for the ladies' expensive drinks with his credit card when he already skipped two instalments on his car? Who was he to judge?

Ten minutes later, Aya came back into the sitting room. Intle was still in the bedroom. All of a sudden there was the noise of a key scraping in a lock and the front door burst open. Sami entered, panting. Surprisingly she was wearing a pair of sunglasses. She was followed by two guys who immediately locked the door behind them. One of the boys had a gold tooth.

"Are we ready, guys?" Intle's voice came from the bedroom.

"Yes, we are ready," answered Aya as she looked at Sami and smiled smugly.

Fana and Sanele started to stand up, but the two guys pushed them back onto the sofa violently. At that moment, Intle came out of the bedroom. She carried a gun in her right hand and a handbag in her left.

"Okay, guys, listen up. We are going to play a little game here," Intle said, throwing her handbag on the table. "First, you give me your car keys and cell phones."

"What?" Fana and Sanele said almost at the same time. "I thought we . . ."

"Stop thinking and do as you are told," Aya said maliciously, putting one foot up on the coffee table.

"Come on, guys, what's happening?" Sanele asked, looking anxiously at Fana.

"You think this is a fucking joke, don't you?" Aya said threateningly. Leaning forward, she opened the handbag and pulled out two pairs of handcuffs. "Well, it's not. Cuff yourselves before my friends here do it for you."

Fana glanced right and left nervously. "But, guys, I thought we were friends," he said, trying to keep his voice light.

"Whose friend do you think you are?" said Intle, cocking the gun. "Do you see us laughing here?"

At that moment Sanele's cell phone rang. Instinctively he knew it was Gontse, his fiancée. He looked at Aya imploringly and then reached into his jacket pocket with unsteady fingers.

"Stop that! What the fuck do you think you're doing?"

Sanele froze; Aya's body radiated the threat of violence.

"Please! This is urgent, ladies. It's my fiancée," Sanele said in a low voice. "She wants to know about the catering people that I need to pay." To Fana it sounded as if his friend were saying the words in a dream.

"Hand that damn thing over or she will put a bullet in you," Aya instructed curtly, gesturing at Intle.

"But she..."

"I said hand it over," Aya repeated.

Sanele hesitated for a few seconds, then he pulled the phone from his pocket. He looked nervous.

"Give it here," Sami ordered.

As Sanele reached out to hand over his phone, Fana snatched at it, knocking it out of his friend's grasp. "I'm not going to let you have it," he yelled, jumping to his feet as the phone clattered onto the coffee table. "You can't do this to us!"

At that moment Intle struck Fana a blow to the head with the butt of her gun. As he doubled over in pain, Aya struck him in the face with the handcuffs. Fana fell down panting. He felt as if he had been struck by lightning.

Seeing what was happening to his friend, Sanele began to sob like a child. Tears were running freely from his eyes and he was trembling as if suffering from a bout of malaria.

"I'm telling you this for the last time," Aya said, malice glittering in her hard eyes. "You must cooperate or else you die."

"No, please. Let us go, please," pleaded Sanele. "I am getting married next week. I beg you, please, take whatever you want."

"Shut up! What do you know about marriage?" Aya said contemptuously. "Let me tell you something, marriage is just pretence. I've been married three times. You know what happened? The same thing every time! Men and their other women! So, don't tell me about marriage and getting married. You know where my last husband is now? I killed him. He is in hell! And that is where you're going too if you don't start cooperating."

Sanele didn't resist as Sami started to search him. She took his wallet, which contained his cards, and his car keys. Satisfied that she had emptied Sanele's pockets, Sami began searching Fana for his keys, wallet and cell phone. The clock on the wall ticked with empty urgency.

As soon as Sami had Fana's bank cards and car keys, Aya handed a pen and paper to Sanele.

"Write down your pin numbers. And don't try to be smart because we will kill you. You will never see your families again, understand?" Aya waited for Sanele to nod. "After that your friend will also give you the pins for all his cards. And don't forget to write the name of the bank with each code."

Sanele nodded. His hands were trembling.

"Next time we won't be so kind," Aya said with triumph in her eyes. "You must cooperate here."

After Sanele had written down their pin codes, he and Fana were handcuffed and thrown into an empty room. The door was locked behind them.

A few minutes later they heard music coming from the sitting room, but, despite this, Sanele and Fana could still hear their captors talking. Aya sounded unhappy with Sami.

"What took you so long? We nearly lost the target."

"I had to get these guys and they were in a nightclub."

"But I told you to be quick when we were still at the restaurant. You know these rich guys have tracker devices on them."

"I'm sorry. It won't happen again," one of the boys said. "I was speaking to the guy who bought the Golf we had last week."

"You bet it won't happen again. You boys need to get it together. Now stop staring at me like that and do what you're paid for," Aya commanded. "Take the keys and drive both cars to the workshop. I want you back here in less than an hour. There is a lot to be done."

"Come on, let's move."

There was the sound of a door opening and shutting somewhere in the house.

"What should we do with them?" they heard Sami ask as first one engine and then another roared into life outside the house.

"These ones have seen our faces. They have to die. Otherwise they will alert the police."

Sanele's forehead wrinkled and fear leapt into his eyes. He searched Fana's face, but his friend's eyes were glazed. It was as if his mind had shut down; he couldn't process what was happening to them.

"I think you're right," Intle said. "That disused mine shaft in Riverlea is the right place. It's about one and a half kilometres deep. No one will find them there."

Those were the last words Fana and Sanele heard from their captors that day. The tears coursed down Sanele's cheeks as they awaited their fate. Fana was silent and withdrawn.

"It is my fault," said Fana after a long time.

Sanele didn't answer.

PASSPORT AND DREADLOCKS

Three days before we left for Zimbabwe, bad luck hit our friend Two-Boy. First, he was robbed of his passport at knife-point. Second, he was robbed of his dreadlocks. It happened on the same night along Twist Street in Hillbrow, not far from Berea, where he lived. He'd had those dreadlocks for about eleven years. They were very long, thick and well cared for. These incidents nearly cost us our trip to Victoria Falls, which we'd been planning for ten months. Each of us had contributed five hundred rands every month to a bank account we'd opened in February. Our friend Herb had been chosen to manage it.

It was Herb's idea that we go to Vic Falls that December, and that we start saving money. Herb had convinced Two-Boy, Sledge and me that many Europeans, especially from Scandinavian countries, visited Victoria Falls during November and December, when it was winter in their countries. He said that Europe is icy and dark around that time, and that most lonely European women come to Africa, and especially to Vic Falls. We believed him. Anyway, Herb had been to different countries, including the United States and England. He told us that European women are fascinated by African men with dreadlocks. This encouraged each of us to grow our dreadlocks before the trip. I had been growing mine for eleven months and they were now as long as my middle finger. Herb had very long ones that ladies loved to touch when we visited taverns in Hillbrow and Berea. He had had them for the past seventeen years, he said. Sledge's dreads were almost the same length as mine.

Three days before we left on our romantic adventure, Two-Boy's dreadlocks were stolen. We only knew about it a day before our journey, on 15 December. As the organiser of the trip, Herb had called each of us that day to confirm the time of our departure. We had planned to leave at four in the morning. Herb's logic was that, since we were travelling northeast, we had to leave before the sun came up. He said that, as the driver, it was better to avoid the morning sun that would be facing him. The truth was that his white Ford Focus didn't have a sunshield. It broke about two years ago and he never fixed it.

On the morning of 14 December, Herb and I tried to call Two-Boy several times. His cell phone was always on voicemail. At about three in the afternoon we decided to drive to his one-bedroom apartment, at the corner of Twist and Pretorius streets. After several knocks he finally opened. He had no dreadlocks. His head was covered with stubble. It made me laugh.

"And now, what do you call this?" Herb asked, looking Two-Boy squarely in the eye. "What happened, Jah-man?"

"I got robbed yesterday," he answered, licking his lips as if trying to get rid of a bad taste.

I listened to him with my finger to my mouth to avoid laughing. He sounded depressed, and his eyes looked heavy and tired.

"No, I mean your dreadlocks, Jah-man," said Herb, pointing at Two-Boy's badly shaven head.

Two-Boy ran his hand over his head.

"They took my money, bank cards, passport and dreadlocks."

Herb laughed, one of his eyes glowing brighter than the other.

"How could that happen?" I asked, genuinely intrigued. "I know they do rob people of their money and passports, but not hair."

"That's what happened. People steal anything nowadays here in Jozi."

"But how did it happen?"

Two-Boy's eyes glinted, and I had to drop my head to hide my grin. I knew that dreadlocks were fashionable, and that Joburg hair stylists would buy them for big cash. But I didn't think they could steal them from one's head. I also heard that drug dealers preferred to use drug mules with dreadlocks because it was easier to hide drugs in them. Not so long ago, a South African girl had been stopped in some international airport with cocaine hidden in her dreadlocks.

"You're not making any sense, Jah-man," said Herb again, sounding as confused as I was.

"I came out of the club drunk. All of a sudden four guys who spoke Shona produced knives. They stuck them on my throat and chest." He touched below his left breast. "They took me to an alley behind a run-down building, searched me and took my wallet and passport. One took a pair of scissors from his pocket. I thought he was going to stab me with it, but I was relieved and surprised when he started to cut my hair. It took about three minutes. Then they kicked me before they ran away with my dreadlocks. Now I don't have my cards, cell phone, driver's licence or my passport."

"Oh fuck," I said as I noticed Two-Boy's swollen ear.

Two-Boy had sweated to get his South African passport. I went with him to Home Affairs in Wynberg on the day they gave it to him, in 2008. He was originally from eMakhandeni Township in Bulawayo, Zimbabwe. His real name was Thulani Dlodlo, but we called him Two-Boy. He had been in South Africa since 2000, and had a scrapyard in Alexandra Township where he fixed cars. That's where I first met him. I'm from 3rd Street, not far from the scrapyard. I remember that in February 2009, six months after he got his passport, the British government announced that South Africans would need a visa from that year to travel to the UK. They said that until something they called biometric security was added to our passports, South African Home Affairs could not be trusted. This happened after thousands of passports had gone missing from different Home Affairs offices around the country. I was watching television with Two-Boy in his scrapyard when the British High Commissioner said that the British were concerned about the security of South African passports and wanted to strengthen their borders against infiltration by terrorists. Now that he had lost his passport, I could read the anger in Two-Boy's face as he told us about the unfortunate incident.

"Which means, guys, my trip to Vic Falls is cancelled," he said sadly, and ran a hand over his face as if washing without water. "I have no choice."

"What are you saying now?" Herb asked, a shadow of disappointment flitting across his face. "There's no way, Jah-man. We have been planning this trip for almost a year now."

Two-Boy shook his head and did not answer for a while. He

sighed in resignation and folded his arms across his chest. Herb frowned.

"But I have no choice, guys," he repeated, as if he felt no one believed him. "I don't even have a passport anymore. I can't apply for one now because it takes three weeks or a month."

"Oh, Jah guide, but we agreed that the money is non-refundable," said Herb gently. He started to cough and then tried to hold it in.

"Well, you'll have to refund me my five grand, guys. It was beyond my control," insisted Two-Boy.

"No fucking way, Jah-man," I said, unable to mask my irritation. "We have already budgeted for the money. And besides, we are leaving tomorrow at dawn."

Two-Boy opened his eyes, narrowed them more than usual, and said, "Sorry guys, you have to cancel it if that is the case and give me my five grand. I can't leave without a passport, never mind my dreads."

Both Herb and I looked at him, and he simply shrugged his shoulders. Herb was quiet for a while and eyed Two-Boy inquisitively. After some mental debating of the point, he came to a conclusion.

"Don't worry. Jah guide, I've got a plan for your passport," he said, giving a wide, naughty smile.

"What's the plan?" I asked.

"There is a guy I know who will leave for Zim only on Christmas Eve," he said as he met my eyes joyfully, baring his gleaming teeth. "He stays here in Hillbrow and his name is Hambo Nsele. I can borrow his passport and you can use it. Jah guide, he looks just like you without the dreads."

I laughed at the idea, as I considered it stupid. Herb started to roll a joint. Two-Boy's face had a frightened expression.

"So you want me to be arrested and sent to jail for a long time? You want me not to see my family at Christmas?"

"Borders are the creation of Europeans to control black people's movements, Jah-man," he said, shifting his eyes from the joint he was rolling. "You know those Europeans have no sense of a big and communal life. Jah guide, I have families here in South Africa, Zambia, Malawi and Zimbabwe. Why should I have those stupid papers to see my families? Bob Marley said we must emancipate ourselves from mental slavery. None but ourselves can free our minds."

"I hear you. But that is or was Bob Marley's ideal world. It's not what Mugabe and Zuma have in their minds. They will lock me in jail if I use someone else's passport."

"Not in Beitbridge," he said, licking the edge of the rolling paper. "Jah guide, I have lots of friends on both the South African and Zimbabwean side."

"There's no way, Jah-man! I'm not going there."

Herb finished rolling the joint, and then lit it. He took a long, hard drag, holding the smoke in.

"Okay, here is a deal. I get that passport and we go tomorrow morning. Jah guide, if you don't cross the border I will give you my car, and it's yours," he said, and his face appeared through the swirls of smoke as he puffed. "You can turn back. Myself, Seed," pointing at me, "and Sledge will continue the journey to Vic Falls by bus while you take the car as yours. That's only if you can't cross the border. And I'm sure you will."

Two-Boy and I laughed at the suggestion. Herb passed the joint to Two-Boy after he gave three rapid nods. Two-Boy took the joint but eyed Herb suspiciously.

"I'm serious, guys. You will cross that border. I tell you that borders are the beginning of the Promised Land, my friend, and not the end of things," said Herb as Two-Boy puffed out smoke through his nostrils. "Money talks in this world. All they will do at the border is to stamp your passport. Jah guide, there will be thousands of people crossing. Do you think officials have all the time to look at an individual person? Hell no. Jah guide, this is Africa, my friend."

When the joint was finished I knew we were all high. There was a moment of utter stillness that I wished would go on forever. Two-Boy never stopped smiling and I'm certain that his mind was already in Vic Falls. Herb just clenched his teeth and closed his eyes. I was standing by the balcony, and sank deep into my thoughts as if listening to the sounds of the cars below on the street.

The following morning at half past four we headed for the N1 North freeway. It was 538 kilometres from Joburg to Beitbridge. Herb was driving and doing the talking. Beside him was Two-Boy. I was with Sledge in the back. Hambo, the person that Herb had to collect the passport from, had slept over in Sunnyside, Pretoria. We had to meet him somewhere along the Steve Biko Road.

"You'll see, guys. I'm not exaggerating," said Herb as we passed Melrose Arch. "Like I said, we don't even have to book the hotel at Vic Falls. Jah guide, we'll sleep in the car for a day or two. Then we'll go hunting for white women, or they will be hunting for us.

There is a place called Hunter's Club, and the other club that white women frequent is inside the Victoria Hotel. Jah guide, there will be white ladies galore. All we have to do is smile at them and drink beer. Yes, they will buy you lots of beers."

"But I don't have dreads, how are they going to even look at me?" asked Two-Boy jokingly, and his expression was perfectly tranquil.

"Don't worry about the dreads, Jah-man. There will be enough for everyone. Like I say, we don't have to book a hotel because it will be a waste. But for you, Two-Boy, we can book you a tent at one of the hotels. Jah guide, that's just in case you take time to get laid because of your missing dreads. The tent is very comfortable but the problem is that the toilets and showers are outside."

"Oh shit," I said.

When we got to Sunnyside, Herb stepped out of the car to talk to a tall guy in the McDonald's parking lot. Sledge was busy rolling joints for us.

"If that is the passport guy, he doesn't look like me at all," said Two-Boy looking at the man talking to Herb.

"He doesn't have to, man," assured Sledge while licking the end of the paper. "Any Zimbabwean passport is safe."

"You think so?"

"Of course I do. Once you have a Zim passport, it automatically means that you don't do fraud. The problem is when you have a South African passport and you're a Zimbabwean. Then you become a suspect. The authorities know that many Zimbabweans fake to be South Africans. The other day I was stopped because I'm dark and suspicious-looking. They asked me to count from one to ten in Afrikaans. They know that people who are not originally from Mzansi can't count in Afrikaans."

"Did you count?" I asked.

"Of course I did," he said, lighting a joint. "You know how brutal the South African police are. I would be dead by now if I didn't."

"It is sad that white people are living comfortably and are not asked such stupid things. We owners of the land are always suspected of being foreigners in our motherland. A criminal can easily come here from Croatia, for example, and get a passport easily. On the streets police won't ask him anything because he is white. Whites are not suspicious in the eyes of our law because of their skin colour."

"That's my point exactly!" said Two-Boy. "That's why you need a visa to go to Britain. But the British don't need a visa to come to our country. It's bullshit. Fucking colonialism! That's why I like Mugabe. He tells these fucking colonialists to their faces that this is Africa. He is not as pretentious as South Africans, who are afraid of telling Europeans that they are foreigners and they must fuck off the land."

By then, Herb and Hambo had come over to the car. Hambo greeted us casually and left. We drove off in the direction of Hatfield. Herb and I were smoking the joints that had been passed by Two-Boy and Sledge. Two-Boy was busy looking at the passport, and especially the photo in it.

"Hambo just came back the day before yesterday. He was in Zim," said Herb without being asked.

"I'm not concerned that he just came back from Zim. But he fucking doesn't look like me at all," said Two-Boy.

"Don't worry, Jah-man. It doesn't matter who he looks like," assured Herb. "Jah guide, the car is still yours if we can't cross over to Zim with you."

Herb tossed the finished joint through the window as we joined the N1 North. Culture's "International Herb" was playing. I was looking at Hambo's picture in the passport, which Sledge had just handed to me. Indeed he didn't look like Two-Boy, but I decided to keep my opinion to myself.

"You'll see when we get there. We'll be drinking and sleeping with white women from Europe and will not need to book a hotel. Who knows?" Herb paused and pointed at Two-Boy. "You might as well get married to a white woman soon and leave for Europe, although it's fucking cold there. Jah guide, you might be lucky and end up getting a very rich divorcee, or a widow, or a young fresh thing."

"Nonsense," I said. "Let's just say we are going to have great fun."

"The world is a possibility if only you'll discover it, my friend. Victoria Falls is a place of dreams and realities. It is the Promised Land," said Sledge, expelling a plume of smoke. "Vic Falls is not a place, my friend. It's a dream, a heaven."

We passed Polokwane City at about half past eight. Stopping at a garage to refuel, we also bought four pies and coffees. The petrol attendant directed us to the bottle store on Dahl Street, but he was not sure if it was open yet. Herb suggested that we buy booze in Musina, which was about two hundred kilometres ahead. We drove along.

"I have a friend called Mlindeli, who ended up marrying this girl from Norway," Herb continued after sipping his coffee and putting the cup between his thighs. "Two years ago I visited him in his mansion in Stavanger. Mli lives like a king, I tell you. He even has a white maid. He has five beautiful coloured kids who speak only Norwegian and English. No fucking Ndebele, no. He got the lady in 2001, and like a true African he has impregnated her five times already. The eldest is only eleven. Jah guide, he was nothing in Zim before, but now he visits Nkulumane Township with a hired Range Rover. Thanks to his dreadlocks, now he has a PhD in anthropology, I tell you. It is so strange that people call him 'professor' now, and he was just a mampara like me some few years ago."

By the time we arrived in Makhado we were so hungry that we decided to drive through the KFC to buy a bucket of chicken and mini-loaves. "Woman, I Love You" by Burning Spear was pumping through the speakers. Musina was just ninety-five kilometres away.

"So, why didn't you get one for yourself?" asked Two-Boy as he started to wind down the window. "You didn't have dreadlocks then?"

"I had a beautiful thing, my friend. I mean my friend Mli had an ugly one, but she was stinking rich. He had made a good calculation. Mine was young and beautiful, but not rich. Jah guide, she was still a university student," he chuckled softly, wrinkles forming at the corners of his eyes. "She could not even afford to pay for my air ticket to visit her, while Mli got a business-class ticket. Last year when he visited Zim, I inquired about my Lisa. He told me that she was married to some black dude from Ghana." He paused. "Shit! Just wait. You'll see when we get there that Vic Falls is the Promised Land."

I listened with fascination. My eyes were glued to the white line dividing the highway, and my thoughts swept back in time. We stopped at the Spar liquor store in Musina to buy some booze. Herb suggested that we get four bottles of Bell's whisky, six bottles of wine and three cases of Windhoek Lager, which was what I preferred. We also added a few packets of biltong, cigarettes and four five-litre bottles of water. The total came to about three thousand and some few rands. From there we drove the last fifteen kilometres to the South Africa-Zimbabwe border. Peter Tosh's "African" was playing.

We saw the Limpopo River Bridge almost at the same time as a flock of birds sailed up and crossed the river from Musina to the Zimbabwean side. We saw people throwing coins into the river for good luck.

There was a long queue at the passport checkpoint. About six buses had just offloaded passengers before us, and they beat us to the queue. The queue moved very slowly. The sun was very hot, and some people unfurled umbrellas in front of us. On the pavement a woman was breastfeeding a baby, revealing old, sagging breasts and hair under her armpits. Perspiration coursed down her left cheek. Not far from her was an old man who kept shaking his head. He had a thin, wrinkled sunburnt neck, and constantly munched his toothless gums.

The public toilets on our right smelt badly. Several small-time businesspeople who claimed to know the officials were busy advertising their services. They were asking people in the queue to give them their passports to be stamped, for a fee of ten US dollars or a hundred rands. Some were looking for people without passports to take them over the Limpopo River, which looked a bit full. Some were selling US dollars at exorbitant rates.

"There's no need to change our rands into dollars because you can use rands anywhere in Zim," said Herb who was behind me in the queue. "What's the use? I mean Zimbabwe is the only country in the world that uses three foreign currencies – rand, dollar and pula. Jah guide, you can buy in US dollars and get change in rands or pula, whichever is available on the till at the time."

"You know what happened to me once? Some motherfucker just across the bridge robbed me of three thousand rands," said Two-Boy. "That was way back in 2006. The bugger promised me a nice deal of six rands to one dollar exchange. I gave him my three grand, and it was in the evening. While I was still counting the dollars that he had just given to me, the motherfucker ran away. I realised later that it was all counterfeit. I had to turn back to Mzansi and could not go home."

"So being robbed is your thing," said Sledge. "Just don't forget that you're no longer Thulani Dlodlo. Consider Thulani dead from here onwards. For seven days you will be known as Hambo Nsele. Hambo Nsele. Hambo Nsele! Remember that."

Seeing that the queue was still long, Herb and I decided to go back to the car to get the drinks. A breeze came through the trees, blowing up piss stink from the toilets. Inside the car, Herb made a joint and we smoked quickly. By the time we came back the queue was more promising. Two-Boy and Sledge had bought boiled peanuts from a woman who was selling them at ten rands a cup. The pavement where we were standing was now littered with peanut shells. They had bought four cups. After giving Herb and me our share, Sledge and Two-Boy left the queue to smoke a joint in the car.

While we were standing there, the immigration office closed for about an hour and a half. An arrogant-looking official was shouting at people, telling them to form a straight line if they wanted help. He threatened to close the office indefinitely if they failed to comply. Thirty minutes later, the official was still arguing with the people to behave. It was then that Herb volunteered to monitor the crowd, and the officer agreed. There were several complaints about people who had jumped the queue, and Herb responded by telling those responsible that they would not be helped unless they went back to their places.

The queue dragged on for about two hours. Not one voice could be distinguished above the noise. Another bus pulled up, disgorging a crowd that sprinted to join the queue. Five hours later, we were almost at the door of the immigration office. After nominating one of the men behind us to take over as queue marshal, Herb collected our passports and gave them to the official behind the counter. The official, who recognised Herb as the queue marshal, lifted his head as if counting us. He didn't ask questions, but stamped all four passports before thanking Herb for maintaining order. We went to the other queue where Herb submitted the car papers. This didn't take long, and a few minutes later we were on our way back to the car, smiling and holding on to our passports. But we were not done yet. We still had to get through on the Zimbabwean side.

We drove towards the five South African officials who were standing at the gate separating the South African and Zimbabwean sides. Herb's car had South African number plates. The officials stopped us and demanded to see our passports and the car papers. Another official called in the number plate of the car on his walkie-talkie.

"It looks like it is going to rain today," said Herb to the officer who was busy checking our passports and looking at our faces.

"Maybe at night," said the officer. "What do you have in the boot?"

"Nothing, officer, it's just our clothes."

"What else do you have?" he asked, scanning inside the car.

"It's nothing else but clothes. We are going to the wedding of my sister, Snini. Mafikizolo will be performing live. You see, if you were not at work, officer, I would invite you to Bulawayo now," he said. "Jah guide, it's happening that side, I tell you, and I would make sure you're on my VVIP guest list."

"Are you serious?"

"I'm telling you. There will be plenty of booze and ladies. And you see, we have space for one more person in the back."

"So where is the cooler box with cold beer?" he asked.

"We don't have. We will buy that side."

"You guys are not serious," he said, smiling. "Why travel such a long journey without a cooler box?"

The official laughed at his own joke. By then the one with the walkie-talkie had finished clearing the car. He signalled for us to go in order to ease the traffic behind us.

"Next time, baba," said the official as he handed us our passports. "Bring a gift for me when you come back."

"I will do. Jah guide."

Ten minutes later we were on the Zimbabwean side. The passport queue was not as long. What was amazing was that the South African side used scans and computers, while on the Zimbabwean side it was mostly manual typing. But it was faster on the Zim side. Herb joked with one of the officers in Shona, and they let us go within two hours.

It was already past eight in the evening when we left Beitbridge via the A6 to Bulawayo. We stopped to refuel at a garage on the left where there were some fried chicken and pizza shops. While we were filling up, Sledge said he wanted to open a beer. Herb warned him about the tollgate and soldiers ahead, and that the police on the Zimbabwean side might be fussy.

The tollgate was before the Masvingo-Harare T-junction. It was just two oil drums on either side of the road and a boom gate in between. We had to pay one US dollar to pass, which fortunately Herb had on him. The signboard in front of us said *Bulawayo 323 KM* with an arrow to the northwest. Another arrow pointed northeast with the words *Masvingo-Harare 585 KM*. We took the northwesterly direction, and came to another sign that said *Gwanda*. I saw only one letter on the signboard, as the others had faded away. We stopped immediately after that sign to pee by the side of the road and also to take some beers out of the boot. Sledge was rolling a joint for us. Bob Marley's "Who the Cap Fit" was playing loudly from the speakers. Outside, the night was so dark that I could not see my own hand in front of my eyes. Sledge lit the joint.

We drove at a hundred kilometres per hour. Insects crushed themselves against the windscreen, leaving yellow mucus smears.

I was already feeling sleepy before we reached Gwanda. Herb dangled his right hand out the window and let the joint drop. Sparks flickered on the road. Then he pointed at a dark village where there was a small glimmer of light.

"That is the school where the Nobel Peace Prize winner Chief Albert Luthuli used to go," he said. I was not interested as I was about to fall asleep. "Jah guide, Zimbabwe brought him up to lead South Africans out the Babylon system of apartheid, just like Moses was raised by the Egyptians to deliver the Children of Israel from slavery in Egypt."

"Yah man," I heard Two-Boy respond. "So Luthuli was a Zimbabwean?"

I woke up when the lights of Bulawayo came into view. A donkey had been run down by a car, and the bloated carcass lay by the side of the road. We drove slowly to avoid hitting any animals. It was about two in the morning. Herb dropped Two-Boy and me at Makhandeni Township near the Woza Woza shops. Two-Boy's mother and two sisters were happy to see us. Herb and Sledge proceeded to the nearby Luveve Township.

In the morning, the jacaranda trees around Bulawayo were in purple bloom. We set off at about seven to buy some isitshwala and nkukhu makhaya, traditional cooked chicken, for our road trip to Victoria Falls. Herb took us to a place he knew called Dickies, in the middle of the city, where we bought two full chickens and isitshwala. As soon as we drove out of the city, the sign on the road said *Victoria Falls 438 KM*. Though we had not had enough sleep, we were in that special state of high spirits and carefree merriment. We listened to Peter Tosh's "Don't Look Back" blasting on the speakers. Before the road split to Nyamandhlovu there was a one-dollar tollgate like the one outside Beitbridge.

The trip to Victoria Falls was uneventful except that we were drinking all the way. I admired the many massive baobab trees that lined the road. Just before the Victoria Falls airport there was another roadblock. This time the police stopped us and we had to pay the bribe because Sledge and I were not wearing seatbelts in the back seat. I was also wearing camouflage shorts, which was apparently not allowed in Zimbabwe. It took us about ten minutes to negotiate, with Herb doing all the talking in Shona. On either side of the road were heavily armed soldiers. I was very worried about Two-Boy's fraudulent passport, but luckily he was also carrying his Zimbabwean identity document.

We arrived at Victoria Falls at about half past eleven that morning. We found a parking spot outside the Spar, next to the rest camp, and then fell asleep in the car until hunger woke us up at about two in the afternoon. On our way to buy food at the Spar, we were stopped by two beautiful young ladies, who gave us pamphlets and told us about the sunset boat trip along the Zambezi. We all felt it was a good idea, and so we followed the ladies to their office inside the complex. After paying a discounted fifty-five dollars each, we were given the cruise vouchers.

At five in the afternoon we boarded the *Pamusha* for the two-hour sunset cruise along the Zambezi River. We sat next to three young white ladies who were speaking a language we did not understand. In front of us were cans of Windhoek Lager offered to us for free during the cruise. The guide on the microphone was telling us the history of David Livingstone, the missionary. We listened as he told us about how Livingstone discovered the place, and about the width of the river, which he said was two kilometres, and its three channels.

We cruised slowly. There were finger snacks, beer, wine, champagne and soft drinks. The young lady next to Sledge tried to open a can of Heineken, but her nails were too long. Shrugging, she passed her beer can from one hand to the other as if it was too cold. She wrinkled her nose and put the can down in frustration. She had two earrings in one ear, three in the other and two rings in her nose. I watched her as she rubbed her knees and looked past me. Conscious of Sledge's scrutiny, she caught him staring at her and smiled. Then she handed the unopened can to him. Without a word, he opened it and gave it to her. The sunlight radiated brilliantly from her long brown hair as she gazed at the hippos ahead. Cameras clicked. One of the ladies asked for a group picture of her and her friends with hippos in the background.

That evening, after the cruise, we went to the Hunter's Pub and partied until late. Inside, our eyes made a swift, anxious scrutiny of the young women there. The light and the noise of the bar held the three prostitutes at the doorway for a few moments. One of them was dressed in a revealing miniskirt. Taking a step towards Sledge and me she began to slide her hands up and down her hips. Then she whispered to both of us, offering herself for a hundred rands or thirty dollars. We ignored her, though Sledge was tempted to take her to the nearby bushes. The girls were from as far away as Zambia, Malawi and Harare. There was also a great number of unattractive single white ladies dancing individualistically.

That first night we slept in the car, in the parking lot behind the rest camp and lodges. It was very uncomfortable, as the mosquitoes buzzed around us the whole night. We had forgotten to close the back window properly before we went to the pub. The night was very hot, such that we had to open the windows. Sledge and Herb snored so loudly that it was difficult for me to sleep. I had to wake up and walk around the car a bit. I only managed to catch an hour's nap at about five in the morning when people were already moving about the streets.

Three baboons were sitting on the roof of a stationary car not far from ours when we woke up. Two white women and a Japanese couple were taking pictures of them. Then three more white ladies and a man jogged over and stopped to admire the relaxing primates. I heard a man's voice chasing the baboons away, and he looked like the owner of the car.

Herb suggested that we go and smoke by the Falls. On our way there, we stopped to buy small bottles of water from a pimple-faced teenager whose thin and stretched upper lip barely covered his protruding upper teeth. Next to him was a stone bearing the words *Welcome to Mosi-oa-Tunya, Victoria Falls, Zimbabwe.* Herb and Two-Boy paid only five dollars each at the entrance as they were Zimbabwean citizens. Herb tried to negotiate for me and Sledge, but never succeeded. We paid ten dollars each.

Herb knew the place very well, and he suggested that we start at the seventy-three steps. There were some old couples taking pictures by the bronze statue of David Livingstone. Herb offered to take a picture of the couples together before we descended the steps down to the gorge. The grass was green as it was summertime, and the birds fluttered their wings and sang. The trees were so close together that they formed a deep green wall that was nearly black. Squirrels were climbing the trees as we descended slowly. A few steps below and ahead of us we could hear the voices of women laughing. Herb was walking ahead of us as Sledge was busy rolling a joint. Midway down the stairs we could see three ladies taking pictures of themselves at the bottom of the seventy-three steps. The sound of the Falls below was like the waves of an ocean on a windy day. Ghostly birds were singing among the green leaves. As we came nearer, there was a rustle of wings and a flock of birds took flight before us. We recognised the ladies from the boat cruise.

"Let me take a picture of you three together," Sledge offered.

The lady with the many rings in her ears and nose smiled and gave him a camera. Another one, with a lean, oval, well-sunned face, gave Two-Boy her iPhone. She had an exceptionally wide mouth. I was standing with Herb looking at both Sledge and Two-Boy as they asked the ladies to say "cheese" while they posed.

"You see, my friend, it's always advantageous to flatter rich white women," Herb whispered in my ear. "Jah guide, they are using my strategy now and it works."

"How do you know they are rich?" I asked, holding the unlit joint that Sledge had handed to me before he talked to the ladies.

"It's obvious, Seed. They are white and foreign. Do you think they can just leave their nice homes in Europe and come here if they were not rich? Jah guide, they will never!"

I kept quiet as Sledge and Two-Boy showed the pictures to the ladies. They looked very happy with his job and thanked him. They spoke rapidly in their language, and then left.

"Enjoy the Falls," said Two-Boy as the ladies passed Herb and me on their way up.

As soon as the ladies had disappeared from our view, I lit the joint. After taking a few puffs, I heard the slap of feet coming down. The sound of footsteps sent a lizard on a tree trunk scuttling for safety. It was the couple that Herb had taken pictures of at the David Livingstone statue. I passed the joint to Two-Boy, who also took some quick puffs.

We decided to go and look for another spot to smoke in peace, as the seventy-three steps looked busy that morning. The sun was full up, but the morning air was still sweet. The movement of people had begun around the Falls as we came up. We walked on until the narrow path passed by a stone marked *Horseshoe Falls 95 m*. We met an old couple, the woman holding her man's hand with fierce possessiveness, the one scarcely saying a word to the other.

Spray from the Falls was settling on us as if it was drizzling. The ladies we had met at the steps were standing there taking more pictures. Ahead of us, a flock of birds dipped down, circled, swung up and out as if they were linked together by a magnet. A light wind began to blow, enough to lift the T-shirt of one of the ladies a bit. Sledge wanted to stop and take another picture for them, but Herb and I suggested jealously that he should not look desperate. He waved at them as we passed, and we walked on towards the bridge that separates Zimbabwe and Zambia.

We walked through thick bushes along the marked pathways. Minutes later we stepped off the trail and I could see a fallen tree ahead. Herb pointed at it as the perfect spot for a smoke. As we sat on the dry tree trunk, Herb and Sledge started rolling joints while I watched the swallows fly past. I tried to count and wondered if they were odd or even numbers. They were flying high and low, round and round, and in straight and curving lines. A lizard skittered over the tree trunk as Herb puffed away on the joint he had just lit. I instinctively looked sideways and saw the three ladies approaching. In anticipation, I gulped down the spittle in my throat. Two-Boy and Sledge looked at each other and smiled. The ladies were looking at us intently from less than ten metres away.

"Hey guys, we meet again," the taller one said, and she smiled with her eyes fixed on Herb's face. "Where can we get that stuff?"

He did not answer immediately. Instead he looked up as if watching the mass of white clouds beginning to gather in the sky on the Zambian side.

"You mean the joint?" he asked as if it was no big deal. "Jah guide, I can get some for you guys if you want."

"When, and for how much?" asked the third lady, who had a small scar on her nose.

"It depends on how much you want and when," said Sledge. "We can even get you a sack if you want."

The ladies looked at each other and smiled. The wide-mouthed one was whipping her hair across her face. Her eyes were light blue. The one with the scar was swatting away a fly that was hovering near her ear.

"We just want a bit that can last us for a week," she said as a ladybird crawled over the nape of her neck. "We are only here for six days."

"Okay, one week's supply?" Herb lifted his long, stained index finger. "Okay. Jah guide, give me thirty dollars."

"Thirty dollars?" she asked as she put her thumb and forefinger beneath the loose collar of her shirt and caught the ladybird. "That's expensive."

"That's a good price for the good stuff. Jah guide, in euros that will be twenty-five."

"Is that a tourist price?" the second lady asked, placing her hands on her hips and looking at Herb. "The security guy at our hotel promised to get us at a cheaper price."

"Jah guide, I guess you got yourselves a better dealer, then," he said, blowing some smoke away. "But be careful. They might sell you bad stuff. The joint I'm going to get for you for thirty dollars is the best. Jah guide, it's the kind of stuff that got Moses in the Bible to see the burning bush thinking it was Jah speaking to him. Have a bit of this and tell me," he said, passing the half-smoked joint to one of the ladies.

The ladies laughed. They sat down with us by the tree trunk and smoked. Beyond, on the Zambian side, we could see people walking towards the Victoria Bridge and passport control. One of them began to shout, but her voice struggled against the sound of the crushing water. The lady sitting between Sledge and I had the sickly smell of cheap mosquito repellent. The other lady rolled the ladybird tenderly between her thumb and finger for few seconds before letting it fall.

"Hi, my name is Seed and I'm from South Africa," I introduced myself.

"I'm Oksana from Latvia," said the lady with the many earrings.

"These are my friends Ineta," pointing at the one with the scar, and then to the wide-mouthed one, "and Vita."

"Do you like it?" Herb asked Oksana.

She nodded her head in agreement. She looked at Herb, her eyes searching his face.

"So when are you going to get us the stuff? There is a music band from South Africa, called The Parlotones, and they are playing tonight. We could do with some supply."

"We'll try tonight. Jah guide, say around ten?"

"I don't remember my local number, but we stay at Victoria Falls Hotel." She paused and bit her lower lip with two childish white front teeth. "Please make it happen."

Three brown-breasted barbets flew past us. Oksana's eyes were following the birds above. She looked at Herb and laughed.

"Whose side is God on, anyway?" she asked out of the blue.

"I beg your pardon?" he asked.

"Jah is on your side, precious Empress Divine," said Two-Boy.

"Where do you guys stay?" she asked, pushing her fingers through her hair.

"Rest camp," said Herb.

We were surprised at his prompt answer, since we were sleeping in the car. After some more puffs, we left. The ladies proceeded as if going towards the bridge and we went back. Two-Boy and Sledge were blaming Herb and me for our interest in their girls.

"Guys, I'm telling you. They liked us and not you," said Sledge, and he appeared angry. "They only came because they saw us, and not you. I think we must set out the rules clear that no person must take another's catch."

"I think you are counting your chickens before they are hatched, caught and cooked," said Herb, smiling. "Jah guide, this is Victoria Falls, my friend. It's the place for the lonely hearts, and has lots of surprises if you ask me."

"But the girls chose us. You guys were all out to disturb us," insisted Two-Boy. "We are the ones that took their photos down there."

"Come on, guys," I said. "Those ladies were just being friendly to all of us."

For the rest of the way back I could feel the tension brewing. At some point Sledge and Two-Boy were talking amongst themselves while they walked ahead of us. We ignored them.

"But why did you lie to them that we stay at the rest camp?" I asked.

"Jah guide, did you want me to tell them we slept in the car?"

The street was busy with traffic heading for the Victoria Bridge. The border was loud with the horns of motorists as we came out of the Falls exit. After having lunch at a nearby fish outlet, Sledge and Two-Boy, who were still a bit tense, said they were tired. They insisted that we book a room at the rest camp lodge, so they could take a shower. Herb wanted us to go to the nearby township to buy weed from people he knew there. We agreed that Sledge and Two-Boy should proceed to the rest camp and book two tents for us while I went to the township with Herb. The two of us took the car.

"I tell you, my friend, there is great business here in Vic Falls, Jah guide," he said.

"So the point of our coming here was for you to make money by selling stuff to the foreigners?" I asked.

"Partly I will say yes. Jah guide, the last time I was here I made about two thousand dollars in a week. Can you believe that? That is the money I used to visit Mli in Norway."

We found the weed and came back to the rest camp. Sledge and Two-Boy had booked the tents for about thirty dollars a night for three nights. I took tent DT 6 with Herb, while Two-Boy and Sledge lodged next door in tent DT 7. The tent was only an arm's length high, and I had to bend down to enter it. Hard brown beetles kept thudding against the dull light. We used the communal toilets and showers that were by the bar and restaurant next to the swimming pool.

The sound of live music came from the far end of the camp where The Parlotones were playing. Herb suggested that we go and wait outside the entrance to see if we could spot the girls to give them their weed package. He promised to give me a ten per cent share of all the proceeds of the sale, and I was not supposed to say a word to Sledge and Two-Boy. We took six beers from the car and waited outside. The concert looked like it was going on forever, with revellers shouting approval of every number. The entrance fee was fifty dollars so we didn't bother to go inside. We didn't even know who The Parlotones were. Instead we sold the joints we were carrying, including the ones that were meant for the girls.

We did not see the girls until the next morning when we went for our smoke near the Falls. We stopped by the township to buy more stock while Two-Boy and Sledge went to find the girls at their hotel. We agreed to meet at the spot where we had smoked the previous day. Herb gave Sledge what was left of the weed before we went to the township.

Upon returning, we found them near the Falls with the three girls. From several metres away, I could tell from their weed laughter that they were already having fun. The girls were all wearing shorts and talking about the concert and how they had danced all night. They laughed, rolling their eyes at each other as if they were strangers. Oksana's eyes were bloodshot, probably from a sleepless night and too much weed. They were also happy with the weed that we brought them, and Vita immediately put it in her small pink bag. The weed was in six small plastic bank bags. To avoid the previous day's tension with our friends over the girls, Herb and I sat at the far end of the tree talking about the weed business. I was staring at a weaver bird's nest I had not seen the previous day.

"Tomorrow, guys, we go to Livingstone for lunch?" said Vita, mentioning the town on the Zambian side. "Please don't disappoint."

"We will come pick you up, say around ten," said Sledge. "It's less than twenty minutes' drive from the border. But the queues might be longer. You guys have my South African number that I just wrote to you, don't you? I've roamed it, but I will also buy a local SIM card."

"You two are coming with us too, aren't you?" she asked Herb and me.

I wanted to say yes, but thinking about what happened yesterday I shook my head. Vita brushed hair off her forehead and blew smoke rings.

"I'm sorry, we have something to do in the township," I said, and Herb also nodded at my excuse. "Next time."

Vita gave us a hurt look. Her eyes left mine reluctantly. I was very jealous, but didn't want to misread the cues like we did the previous day. Sledge, Two-Boy and the girls were in the most merry and cheerful spirits. After a smoking session, we walked back. Sledge and Oksana walked slowly in front of us, and he timed his pace to hers. They looked very happy. Her hand was drawn through his arm. It looked as if he feared to detach himself lest Herb and I take her. We walked behind them with Vita. Ineta and Two-Boy walked in a slow swagger behind us.

Oksana and Sledge were now walking quickly, and she took quick short steps towards the gorge. He kept beside her with his long stride. Just as we reached the gorge, we stopped as Sledge tried to take a picture of Oksana. I watched Vita as she shifted her small bag to her other shoulder. The sound of the Falls was very loud. Herb and I watched as Oksana gave Sledge her cell phone. He looked down to adjust the camera before taking a picture of her with the Falls in the background. We resumed our walk, but slowly. Sledge clicked several times at the posing Oksana. Suddenly, she reversed towards the gorge.

"Look out," Herb shouted as Oksana's right hand shot out towards the gorge, posing for a picture.

She kept walking backwards as we shouted. Vita and Ineta also shouted in their language, but Oksana kept on reversing. Then she slipped and disappeared into the gorge. All we heard was a weird squeaky sound, like when a dog is stepped on. My breath was rasping as if I had run a long-distance race or come upon a coiled snake. I watched Vita, and her whole body was shaking with fright. Sledge was holding Oksana's cell phone, with one hand on his head. Ineta's hands were covering her face. Nervously, Sledge and Herb stepped towards the edge of the gorge and looked over.

"Can you see her?" asked Vita, looking at Sledge. "Somebody must dive in to get her!"

"I can't see a thing. It's too far down there," shouted Sledge against the sound of the churning water.

"Oh no," cried Ineta, and she threw her arms round Two-Boy's neck. "What are we going to do now?"

Vita burst into loud, racking sobs. When she had quietened down, Herb handed her a clean tissue that she snatched and slapped against her face. I wanted to be dreaming, but I was there, awake and witnessing death. Herb and I sat by the large stone consoling Sledge, who blamed himself for the accident. Drops of water clung to his forehead. Two-Boy, Vita and Ineta went to report the matter to the Falls management. Herb walked towards the nearby bushes, where he hid the packets of weed. He came back with blackjacks clinging to his pants, as he had cut through the high grass. We started flirting with all sorts of stories, shifting from one extreme situation to another. Sledge blamed the joint, Herb thought she wanted to commit suicide, I thought it was a mistake that she slipped and fell.

Two people from the Falls management arrived, together with two policemen. A number of people had already gathered around the spot. Some were walking along the edge of the gorge to see if they could see anything.

About an hour later we were all taken to the police station. A portrait of President Mugabe hung on the wall of the room where we were told to wait. Minutes later the station commander came in. He asked for our proof of identity and made us write statements. He had an unusually narrow face for a man, and his nose was a bit off-centre. We gave him our passports. Two-Boy produced his Zimbabwean ID instead. The girls were so nervous that Ineta was shivering. Vita's handbag was wedged under her arm. As she took out her passport, a small plastic packet of weed fell out. She was standing so close to me that I could hear her breathing hard. I timed my move and tried to step on the packet. Unfortunately a policeman with acne on his cheeks saw what I was doing. He shot me an angry smile, placed his front teeth over his lower lip, and wiggled an index finger.

"So, you guys were getting high by the Falls, and probably trying to get laid too," said the station commander, looking at me.

He blinked as if to get a clearer view of me. I tried to think, and cleared my throat, but words escaped me. Vita's eyes widened. The station commander opened our passports and read our names out loud.

"Herbert Nhlalo Mjoji, Sidney Ngubo, Thulani Dlodlo and Duma Maseko. You people give Zimbabwe a bad name in Europe," he said threateningly.

He shook his head and took a long swallow of his own spittle, which made his Adam's apple seem unusually sharp-edged, like a blade threatening to cut through his neck. He was a broad-shouldered man, and his neck looked like it was stiff. He looked at Ineta, whose eyes were weak and watery. She licked her lips, and hair tumbled across her forehead as he talked to her directly.

"Is this what you come to Africa to do?" he stood before her and looked at her strangely. "Doing drugs with African boys?"

Mutely, Ineta shook her head as the commander forced a smile to break through the clouds of his feigned anger. She twisted her mouth as if she was smiling shyly and threw wisps of hair from her face. A minute later, the commander and the two policemen leant together confidentially.

"You guys must follow us," said the policeman with the acne cheeks to Sledge, Herb, Two-Boy and me.

That was the last we saw of the two girls, as we were taken to a separate room and locked inside. There was nothing in the room but a single old sponge and a blanket. We were given two slices of brown bread with hot tea for dinner at about four in the afternoon. During the night, the mosquitoes bit us at will. We had to share the one blanket, but luckily it was a hot night. The moths lured by the light fought to die on the glaring light bulb. Beetles crashed drunkenly against the walls. None of us slept. We were bouncing around ideas about the girls.

"What do you think they will do to them?" I asked randomly from one corner of the room.

"Let me see," said Sledge. "They will probably blackmail the ladies into sleeping with them in exchange for their freedom."

"No. This is Zimbabwe. They will probably squeeze some euros out of them," said Herb. "They will not rape them. Jah guide, I don't think so."

"What do you think will happen to us?" asked Sledge.

"Jah guide, money talks. This is Zimbabwe."

"I can't believe Oksana just disappeared like that," said Two-Boy, who seemed to be more hurt than the rest of us.

"Jah guide, I think she was taken by the nyaminyami to be his wife."

"What the fuck is that?" asked Sledge.

"He is the Zambezi River god who lives in the Kariba Gorge. He is still very angry about the building of the Kariba Lake and Dam."

"That doesn't make sense to me. Why would he choose her out of the millions of people that visit this place?" asked Sledge.

"When the Kariba Dam was built in 1956, nyaminyami was separated from his wife by the wall. He decided to kill many construction workers, including the white engineers. Every time he is horny he causes earth tremors as he tries to reach for his wife. Because of the Babylon wall of the dam, he cannot reach her. So he has to swim to Vic Falls to pick a woman. Unfortunately he chose your Oksana."

"Fuck that. She simply fell into the gorge," I said, though I partly believed him.

"I guess wherever she is she must be pregnant by now," said Sledge.

"Jah guide, it is less than a day since she fell."

"He could be right," said Two-Boy. "When I was growing up in Bulawayo I heard stories about this nyaminyami. I heard that he has the body of a snake and the head of a fish."

"And Jah guide, your girl can only come back if you ask the indigenous owners of the Kariba region, the Tonga people, to do a sacrifice to appease him. Otherwise you will never see her again."

"But how do you take a woman against her will? This nyaminyami is a violator of women's rights," said Sledge.

We did not sleep much. At nine in the morning we were again given tea with two slices of brown bread. The officer who brought the food was very sympathetic. Herb even managed to give him fifty dollars to go and buy us food, which was allowed.

At about eleven in the morning the commander came in with Acne Cheeks. We had no idea of our fate as the two entered the room.

"Let's start with you. Do you smoke weed?" the commander asked Sledge, while his eyes roved very slowly all around the room.

"Sometimes."

"Let me see your hands."

Sledge shrugged off the deliberate provocation as the commander examined his hands. His fingertips were stained amber. The commander himself had thick, stubby hands and oversized feet. I shifted my attention to Two-Boy as he started cracking his knuckles and looking at his fingers sadly. The tips of his nails were coal-black.

"Don't lie to me. You smoke every day," the commander shouted at Sledge, and then narrowed his eyes and looked at Herb as he gabbled on, "With you I don't have to ask."

Sweat beaded on the commander's forehead, and his mouth was flecked with foam. He looked at the police officer once, glanced at us, and then looked back at the officer and nodded in agreement. The police officer gave him our passports, which he opened.

"Let me see, which one of you pushed her, according to the ladies?" He pointed at Sledge while holding his passport. "You're a South African without manners. So you are the one that was trying to rob the lady of her cell phone and money?" Then he pointed at Herb and said, "And you were selling the other one dagga."

He spoke the words with real amusement while writing in his notebook. I was dumbfounded with fear and surprise. Sledge squinted in confusion, and Two-Boy's face assumed a distracted and glum expression.

"Is that what they told you?" asked Two-Boy, numbly.

"How do you think we know all this, you idiot?"

"Because it's not the truth," said Two-Boy.

"There are several witnesses against you."

"But, why would they —"

"You'll tell that to the judge next year in March when you appear in court. In the meantime we have a duty to clear our country of criminals like you."

"What? Are we here until next year?" Sledge blurted out.

"That's if you're lucky and don't face a death sentence for killing a foreigner on Zimbabwean soil."

He gave a lead, and the other officer joined in a scornful laugh. I felt like I had just lived in a reality that I let slip away. The shock hit my stomach and nerves, which began to churn around.

"The girl's father was contacted yesterday and he is on the way here. He is a rich guy," the commander said while looking at my passport without interest. "But as we are speaking, the girls are on their way home. Imagine the damage this will do to our country if we let murderers like you out. All that European media will be saying that this country kills white people and that Mugabe is a murderer, especially those British Bum Cleaners called BBC."

After the commander left, we realised the seriousness of our case. I felt trapped with little hope of escape. We fell silent for a long time. Two-Boy sat in the corner, his head in his hands. The officer who had been sent out to buy food came back with a tin of Lucky Star fish and a white loaf. He opened the tin outside and gave us the fish on a plate. He didn't give back any change. We ate in silence. Sledge sat still, his legs crossed and one elbow resting on the folded sponge. His eyes were closed and he looked as if he were asleep. He had no appetite to eat, but Herb forced him. He did so reluctantly.

"Eat, Jah-man. Everything is in Jah's hands, including our lives. Jah guide, we will get out. The dark always has its bright side."

That night we noticed something wrong with Sledge. He was shaking. His lips moved, but I could not hear what he was saying. He completely lost his appetite for the tea and bread, and started throwing up. When the officer who had bought us the food came, Herb gave him money to go and buy fever medicine at the nearby pharmacy, which was fortunately still open. The commander had knocked off for the day. We forced the medication into Sledge's mouth, and he kept gurgling it out. We could not sleep that night.

In the morning the commander came and asked what was wrong, as if we were responsible for Sledge's condition. His eyes were popping out like a dead fish. We thought he was dehydrated and made him drink some mango juice the officer had bought for us. But the juice ran down his chin, staining his shirt. The commander was panicking, and drew in his breath sharply.

"Is he on medication?" he asked.

"We have no idea," said Herb.

"I think he has malaria," said the officer with him. "I have seen the signs. He shivers even when it's hot in here."

The commander called his officer outside. A few minutes later the officer came in alone, licking his lips. He told us that we were free to go on condition that we take Sledge straight to the hospital. He also said that we had to pay a fine of a thousand rands for smoking weed near the Falls. With regard to Oksana's death, we were told we would be called as soon as the investigations were under way. They had our contact details, he said. I don't know whether it was because of Sledge's illness that we were released, but I was happy. Since Sledge was too weak even to walk, Herb went to the lodge to bring over the car.

About thirty minutes later, Herb's arrival was announced by the sound of Jimmy Cliff's "Dear Mother". The officer helped us to lift Sledge into the back seat of the car, which was by now covered with a fine coating of red dust. I sat next to him while Two-Boy and Herb got in front.

"Jah guide, we're out."

"I can't believe those girls sold us out," I said.

We passed by the Spar supermarket to buy ice and water, as well as some mageu for Sledge. He had been rubbing his abdomen weakly with his hand, as if it ached, and we thought this was a sign of hunger. My heart thumped as I groped for the safety belt. Herb shifted the gear lever into third as the road out of Victoria Falls became a bit steeper. Two-Boy was rolling a joint from the weed that Herb had bought in the township before he came to pick us up.

We took the A8 road back to Bulawayo. Sledge's head was

cushioned on my lap. I had taken off his jacket in case he vomited. Only his tired-looking eyes spoke to me. As we drove, Herb kept up a flow of conversation that took our minds away from Sledge's health. It was all about the girls. He and Two-Boy were laughing and talking. I had to lean forward to catch their conversation.

"What a pleasure deferred," Herb said. "Jah guide, you were this close to getting laid."

"Fuck," said Two-Boy while peeling the wet label from a Windhoek bottle. "I have never heard a sound so sweet and dear as that Ineta's voice."

Every time they spoke, I strained my ears to listen. Sledge was groaning on my lap. Herb passed the joint back to me. I smoked it until my fingers burnt, looked at it, and then pulled it away. Sledge's eyes narrowed with every puff I took. His head snapped back as if struck.

"Force him to have two puffs," Two-Boy said, referring to Sledge, whose eyes were half-closed. "The herb will heal him."

"He can't even open his damn mouth."

"Let's burn another joint and make a hot box," Herb suggested. "I'm sure the smell will get into his lungs and heal him."

When the windows were closed the car stank of weed and old takeaway food. I could feel that it was also difficult for Sledge to breathe. The sunshine through the window was painful to my eyes, and I could not even look at the signs ahead or the buildings on the side of the road.

"No guys, hot box will kill him. Let's rather open all the windows," I said.

"Okay, I have an idea. Why doesn't Two-Boy drive and you,

Seed, come and sit here in the front," said Herb as he pulled the car over to the side of the road just before the sign for the Victoria Falls airport.

They both got out. Herb opened my door carefully to let me out. Then he had two puffs from the joint he took from Two-Boy before he took my place in the back. We drove away while I puffed on the joint, before passing it back to Herb. We passed the airport on the right. I watched Herb inhale the smoke before breathing it out on Sledge's mouth. Sledge coughed few times.

"I told you this will work," he said, and laughed between puffs. "Jah guide, the herb is the cure for everything."

"Maybe you must give him mouth to mouth with smoke," said Two-Boy, pinching his lower lip.

"I don't think so, guys," I said. "We must get him to the hospital very soon."

I looked at the speedometer. Two-Boy was driving at one hundred and eighty kilometres per hour. Far down the road, the sun was already glaring cruelly against a sign nailed to a tree. Just after we passed the turnoff to Hwange National Park, there was a roadblock. Two police officers stood in the middle of the lane signalling for us to stop.

"Oh shit. Do you think I must stop?"

"Please stop. There are always soldiers hiding under the bushes with guns. They will shoot us dead if you try to pass."

We immediately opened all the windows to let the smoke out, and Herb threw away the butt of the joint he was smoking. We came to a sudden stop a few metres after the roadblock. Our heads lurched forward and I braced myself against the dashboard.

"Salibonani. Are you guys aware of the speed you've been travelling?" asked the police officer.

"Sorry officer, but we are carrying a sick passenger." Two-Boy pointed at Herb and Sledge in the back. "We are rushing him to the hospital."

"But you're endangering the lives of the people inside the car and those of other road users."

"We understand, officer," said Herb. "But this man is very ill."

"Aha, on top of that you guys are not wearing your seatbelts," said the other officer who had just walked over, a camera in his hand. "We have to take your car."

"But he will die."

"Let me show you the speed recorded by the camera."

The camera had recorded one hundred and eighty-four in a one hundred and twenty zone. The officer glared at Two-Boy and then shot his eyes inside the car. He saw Sledge, whose eyes were half-open. There was a mild expression of anger from him.

"What did you do to him?"

"We think he is down with a bout of malaria and that is why we are rushing him to hospital," said Herb.

"You guys have to go to jail for this. It's way above the speed limit. You're facing a fine of over one thousand dollars and a jail term."

"Please, officers. Let's talk."

Herb searched his pockets. He gave the officer five hundred dollars in folded notes. The officer extended a hand, and took it with the reluctance of a man with wet palms. We waited in timorous silence to hear what he might say next.

"Okay, fine. You must now drive slowly. You're lucky. Otherwise you'd be sleeping in jail."

He looked up at the sun and put on his shades before motioning us to go. It was now past three in the afternoon. Sledge's condition was bad. He was breathing very hard and slow. As soon as the police were out of sight, Two-Boy accelerated to a hundred and sixty. He popped his head in and out of the window every moment.

"Jah guide, I don't think Sledge will make it," said Herb.

"Don't say that," I asked.

There was a moment of silence as I looked in the back. Sledge's eyes and mouth were half-open, but without sign of life. His pupils were white. Bulawayo was just eighty kilometres away. Two-Boy stopped the car by the side of the road.

"Shit, he's not breathing."

"What shall we do if he passes away?"

"Why don't we try to force a malaria pill down his throat?"

We parked under the shade of a tree and opened all the doors. Three squirrels were feeding on the fallen berries of the tree as Two-Boy rolled three joints. I ground two malaria pills in my palm with a bottle cap until they were powder. There were bird calls in the distance as I mixed the powdered pills with water from the bottle. Before we could light the joint, Herb tried to open Sledge's mouth. He was dead.

"No. Jah guide, this cannot happen to us."

We closed the door and propped his body up in the seat and against the window. We supported him with bags that we took from the boot of the car. Squirrels scavenged nervously behind the tree as we sat and smoked in silence, one joint after another.

My mind started to think of the nyaminyami story. Before my eyes, I could see Sledge turning into nyaminyami with Oksana. I also thought about what we were going to tell his parents in Soweto. Sledge was from Zone Two, Meadowlands, just by the police station. I didn't know his family that well. Suddenly our thoughts were drowned out by music from a passing car.

"Please, let's go," I begged.

"Are you mad?" said Two-Boy. "How do we leave in daylight with a corpse inside the car?"

"So how are we planning to do this?"

He thought about it, and rubbed his face. Herb was kicking a tree trunk in anger. I could feel my own eyes misting. The buzz of a large fly was loud in my right ear. Two-Boy was sitting with his back against the tree with his mouth open. It was as if he was listening to distant echoes. A fly stayed on his lower lip, rubbing its forelegs together. Then he swatted it away, and it veered off.

"Let's wait until dark at least," said Herb.

"How about we take him to the mortuary in Bulawayo?"

"That's risky. It will be expensive to transport him to South Africa. There will be a lot of admin and legalities, I warn you."

"But we can buy a coffin and use the malayishas to transport his body."

"We don't have enough money left," said Herb. "We don't even have enough money for petrol. You know the papers that have to be filled in? Besides, we still have the cloud of the criminal case hanging over us in Vic Falls."

"Fuck, but we didn't do anything," I said.

"Not according to the police. And now this will add to our problems," said Two-Boy. "We have to think carefully, guys."

"Two-Boy is right. This may delay our return to South Africa," Herb agreed. "We are in deep shit, guys. What if they say we killed him and Oksana?"

We sat there drinking and smoking as we tried to force the limits of our imaginations to extremes. Herb took a lungful of smoke and tapped his right foot. The sun was turning orange behind the hills when he decided he had an idea. The plan was to drive straight to South Africa without stopping anywhere. Herb convinced us that the border gate at Beitbridge was open twenty-four hours. Then we searched Sledge's bag and took out his sporty hat and shades. Herb put them on Sledge and sat beside him in the back before we drove off.

"Guys, I have a bad feeling about this," I said. "Why don't we put him in the boot?"

"And what do we tell the police at the roadblock if they decide to search the car? They will think we killed him on purpose."

I could not remember what I wanted to say next. Even when I pursued the thought, it eluded me. I could see city buildings looming in the distance. We reached Bulawayo at about half past six. Two-Boy played Burning Spear's "Any River" and Herb bobbed his head until we reached a petrol station. We put in a full tank and drove off. The buildings of Bulawayo rushed at us with human faces blurring past. Ahead of us, I saw a pink and white image of a girl smiling down from the billboard of a Mazoe juice advertisement.

Before Gwanda, we stopped the car. It was my turn to go and sit next to the corpse. We agreed that Two-Boy's turn would be after Gwanda. I twisted a beer bottle open, and with three swallows it was gone. I gazed straight ahead as I opened another. Herb was rolling a joint.

"Jah guide, we'll be at the border before eleven."

"How are we going to cross with the corpse?" I inquired.

"I have no idea," said Herb, before turning to Two-Boy and saying, "Just step on it. Jah guide, we will be out of Babylon."

"Fuck, this is not on," I said.

"Do you have a plan?" asked Two-Boy.

"No. I don't."

"Then stop talking about the corpse."

The highway marker in front of us said it was a hundred and eighty kilometres to the border. My eyes remained glued to the far distance, gazing at the blind side of darkness on the side of the road. Two-Boy was driving with brights on, ignoring the oncoming cars that flashed their lights at us. We were lucky not to hit any grazing animals. Since Two-Boy was driving faster, Herb volunteered to come and sit with the corpse.

We stopped after passing a dark village. The quiet night was broken by the sound of crickets. I was certain that Herb was avoiding the panic that was registering on my face. Before we drove off, Herb opened the boot, took out the four bottles of wine and a half-empty bottle of whisky and sat in the back seat. I watched him open a beer and drink half of it before putting the bottle between the corpse's thighs.

"Fuck, what are you doing?" I asked, confused.

"We'll pretend he is drunk when we arrive at the border. I want this beer to spill on his trousers."

"What the fuck?"

"My father used to work at the mortuary in Tsholotsho. I have seen many corpses in my life."

"Oh shit. Are you serious?" asked Two-Boy, his eyes concentrating on the road ahead.

"I remember this one day, a lady died. She was very beautiful and used to go out with my father's friend, who was a policeman. But they had since separated, and the man was very bitter. So he came to the mortuary where the lady's body was being kept. Jah guide, the poor man asked my father to open the tray for him so that he could see her. You know what happened?"

Two-Boy listened attentively and nodded his head approvingly. I had to lean towards Herb to catch what he said.

"No, tell us," I said.

"Jah guide, the man hit the lady's corpse so hard on the thighs. He cursed her and called her all sorts of disgusting names. He accused her of being a prostitute, and that he was happy she was dead."

"No way, was he normal?" said Two-Boy, giggling.

"I'm telling you. Jah guide, he even went to his car, came with his six-pack of Castle Lager and refrigerated it inside the tray with her corpse."

"That's madness."

"You can say so, but I watched him drink the same beers with my father. Maybe that is what desensitised me about death."

We roared with laughter. We were by now about ten kilometres from the border. We could see the lights of Beitbridge town. Less than a kilometre ahead of us the cars were slowing down as they approached the tollgate.

"I'll do the talking, guys. Jah guide, in Musina, we will stop and find the mortuary. Hopefully, the Zimbabwean guy that works at the petrol station will be doing night shift. He will help us."

We paid the one-dollar toll and drove slowly towards the border. We parked the car in the parking lot. Herb collected our passports and the three of us got out of the car, leaving the corpse inside.

The border post was buzzing with people. From the sky, thousands of stars looked down on us as if they knew that we were carrying a corpse. Doubts and panic crept into me as we walked towards the passport control building. The queue was not that long. Herb made small talk with the border police as we got all the passports stamped. He seemed to know the officer that helped us from his previous visits between South Africa and Zimbabwe.

"So, you guys are gonna sit here the whole night without drinking? That's not acceptable. The night will be very long for you. I have a bottle of whisky left in the car from the wedding."

He told one of the police guys to wait for us, as he was coming with the bottle for him. As soon as we reached the car, Herb asked Two-Boy to sit with the corpse so that he could answer all the questions related to the car. We made sure that the brim of Sledge's hat covered his eyes, as if he were sleeping.

Before the car was even cleared, Herb gave the policeman a bottle of wine and what was left of the Bell's. Another police officer came and flashed the torch into the car. He asked to see what was in the boot, and Herb opened up for him. In the meantime he was busy talking to the police officer to whom he had just given the alcohol.

"We have decided to stop drinking until New Year's Eve," he said, and I could tell he was trying to distract the officer.

"I can see you guys had fun. The sleeping guy must be very drunk with the bottle of alcohol on his thighs."

"It was the greatest wedding," Herb said.

The car was cleared, which left us with the problem of the South African side. We drove slowly over the bridge and parked the car at the passport checkpoint. Herb submitted the passports to the tired-looking officer. He didn't ask many questions. Within an hour, we were gone.

In Musina, Herb stopped at a red traffic light and surveyed the passing traffic. A laughing couple darted across the street, holding hands and wrapped up in each other. They looked as if they were from a nearby pub that was still open. We drove slowly towards the garage. The guy we were looking for was off duty. We asked his colleagues for his number, which they didn't have. Then we asked them to direct us to the mortuary, which they did.

The mortuary was not far away, but it was closed. Luckily there was a contact cell phone number displayed on the wall. We dialled, but no one answered. Herb decided that we would sleep in the car to avoid complications. We parked by the side of the road opposite the mortuary. We drank and smoked while trying to figure out how to confront Sledge's family. None of us had his parents' or relatives' contacts. Herb started to search Sledge's corpse and found a cell phone that was switched off. Fortunately it didn't require a code to unlock it. We wrote down every number that we thought belonged to his relatives.

At about midnight, Sledge's phone rang, and it registered a

foreign number. We hesitated before answering it. When Herb picked it, he put the caller on speaker.

"Hi," said the female voice. "Is that Sledge?"

"Yes, it is."

"Hi Sledge, it's Vita here in Latvia. We have been trying to call you guys since that day in Vic Falls. Are you back from Zimbabwe?"

"Hi Vita. Yes, we are back."

"I hope you guys are not angry with us about the incident at the police station. I don't know what happened and the weed just fell out of my bag. I'm so sorry."

"It's fine. We understand. It was not your fault."

"Did they also make you pay five thousand dollars for being in possession of drugs?"

"What?"

"Yeah, so we had to cancel the trip after all the bad luck and death of our friend. We flew back the following day. I asked my parents to book the ticket for me, and Ineta did the same."

"Sorry about Oksana."

"Thank you. Well, her suicide could not have been prevented. She had her engagement broken off twice. The recent one with Ivo was very bad. We think that might have been the reason. No human intelligence could have read the mysteries of her mind."

"Hang on, but we were told by the police that you guys said that Sledge . . . I mean, that I pushed her?"

"It was all a lie. We didn't say such a thing. We told them she committed suicide."

ACKNOWLEDGEMENTS

"The Warning Sign": A short version of this story was first published as "Between Bela-Bela & Thabazimbi": *Sunday Times*, 27 April 2014.

"Goliwood Drama": First published in *The Obituary Tango*: Jacana, 2006.

"The Dark End of Our Street": First published in Germany as "Auf der Schattenseite": *Yizo Yizo*: Peter Hammer, 2005.

"Betrayal in the Wilderness": First published as an audiobook in Dutch (as "Verraad in de wildernis") and in English in 2009 by *Radioboeken* (http://radioboeken.eu).